DIVORCE

DIVORCE

Hope for the Hurting

FRANK RETIEF

CHRISTIAN
FOCUS

STRUIK

All Scripture quotations, unless otherwise indicated, are taken from the HOLY BIBLE, NEW INTERNATIONAL VERSION. Copyright © 1973, 1978, 1984 by International Bible Society. Used by permission of Hodder & Stoughton Publishers, a member of the Hodder Headline Group. All rights reserved. 'NIV' is a registered trademark of International Bible Society. UK trademark number 1448790.

Scripture quotations marked 'NKJV' are taken from the New King James Version. Copyright © 1982 by Thomas Nelson, Inc. Used by permission. All rights reserved.

Scripture quotations marked 'NASB' are taken from the New American Standard Bible®, Copyright © 1960, 1962, 1963, 1968, 1971, 1972, 1973, 1975, 1977, 1995 by The Lockman Foundation Used by Permission (www.Lockman.org).

Scripture quotations marked 'REB' are taken from the Revised English Bible. Copyright © Oxford University Press and Cambridge University Press 1989.

The case histories in this book are based on real-life experiences and are used with permission of the people concerned. Names have been changed and a few minor facts have been altered to help maintain anonymity.

British Library Cataloguing in Publication Data. A catalogue record for this book is available from the British Library.

© Frank Retief

ISBN 1-85972-421-5
ISBN 978-1-85972-421-3

First printed in 1990
Struik Christian Books ltd., Cape Town, South Africa

Reprinted 1995, 1998, and 2010
by
Christian Focus Publications,
Geanies House, Fearn,
Ross-shire, IV20 1TW, Great Britain

www.christianfocus.com

Cover design by Daniel van Straaten

Printed by
Norhaven A/S, Denmark

Content

Foreword

The erosion of time-honoured values and the rejection of the biblical ethic have played havoc with family life. Single-parent families abound. Thousands of children are deprived of a father and mother figure as they grow up. The cost is incalculable both in terms of economics and heartbreak. Divorces are not cheap either from the perspectives of the divorcees or the state. The break-up of a marriage is traumatic to both parents and kids. Society is increasingly in a mess.

Frank Retief has turned his attention to this chaotic scene. He does so as a pastor as well as a Bible expositor. Crucial to Retief's preaching and books is the death of our Lord Jesus Christ. This volume is no exception. That one can write a book on divorce and maintain frequent reference to the forgiving, healing and restorative power of the cross is proof indeed of an extraordinary evangelistic gift and a commitment to the principle that nothing – even the break-up of marriage – is outside the sovereignty of God.

Retief is refreshingly honest. Divorce is *not* a sin, though the circumstances leading up to it might well be. There *is* life after divorce. The grace of God is a match for human heartache even at its worst. Relentlessly the author pursues his theme. He seems to leave no stone unturned as he cites examples of the human dilemma and then shows how the Bible relates to each issue. He talks straight, not just from the mind, but from the heart. He speaks courageously. Not all marriages can or should be saved. He endeavours to relieve people of unnecessary guilt without watering down the issues. Retief hurts and heals; he makes incisions, performs the surgery and with the stitches of grace closes the wound.

This is not an exhaustive book delving into the minutiae of textual argument. People with marriage problems don't usually reach for such books! What makes this book virtually unique is that it is addressed to the ordinary person. It is eminently readable and biblically reliable. In my opinion it is and will remain a classic of pastoral theology dealing with one of the greatest issues confronting the complex twenty-first century. Men and women do not have to 'watch each other groan.' In Christ there is help, hope and a future. Frank Retief has again served us well.

Dr Tony Sargent
Principal Emeritus International Christian College
Glasgow, Scotland

Introduction

For many Christians, the issue of divorce is shrouded in myths. These wrong beliefs have no basis in truth but prevail in the church and make it more difficult for the believer to recover from the trauma of a divorce experience.

Myth No 1 is: *You won't survive*. The problems are too great; the implications are too overwhelming. What will you do about your sex life and drives? What about the embarrassment in facing your friends? How will you ever forge a new social circle? What about the children? They must have a father and a mother. Above all, there is the utter sadness of losing someone you love – maybe to the arms of another.

It seems as if the emotional overload is just too much. But the truth is, people *do* survive, including children. It may not be easy. There may be wounds and scars. There may be a price to pay. But people *do* survive.

Myth No 2 is: *The only thing the Bible has to say about divorce is don't*. You may think that your standing as a Christian is at stake, but this is also not true. It is true that the Bible is opposed to divorce, but the Scriptures have more to say about divorce and human relationships than most people think. Believe it or not, God is not opposed to *all* divorces.

Myth No 3 follows this closely: *Because the Bible is opposed to divorce, there are no options.* This view believes that when it happens, God simply does not recognise it. The truth is that God does recognise divorce. He condemns murder too, but when it happens, He does not refuse to recognise it on the basis that He has forbidden it. God hates divorce, but He recognises it when it happens.

Myth No 4 says: *Divorce is almost the unforgiveable sin, but to divorce and remarry is definitely not allowed.* That would be adding adultery to my guilt. This may be true, depending on the circumstances, but it is not necessarily so.

Myth No 5 is probably the saddest of all. For many people who do not understand the wonderful power of God to forgive, restore and answer prayer: *Divorce is the only way out.* The truth is, it is not. Hundreds of divorces granted each year could have been avoided. Forgiveness and reconciliation are the better options. Sadly, many people do not know how to start this process. The only alternative is to hang grimly onto their pride, stubbornness and anger, with all the tragic consequences that has.

Divorce is sometimes necessary. This may come as a shock, but it is true. God does *not*, contrary to the belief of some, expect us to stay in a marriage under *all* circumstances. A marriage cannot succeed unless both parties are committed to it and willing to cooperate. Divorce must be the last resort, but it is a resort. However, not even divorce as a last resort can be considered justifiable for a Christian couple until they have looked seriously at the option of reconciliation. We will examine this in the course of this book.

The aim of this book is to offer hope to the hurting. All real hope must be built on truth.

The truth about divorce

Writing about a subject as controversial as divorce opens the possibility of people misconstruing what has been said. Some may assume that I am advocating divorce or at least making it easier than the Bible permits. A few words are therefore necessary to enable the reader to maintain a truly biblical perspective on the issue.

I believe that the Bible, the revealed and inspired word of God, teaches that God hates divorce (Mal. 2:16). So do I, and so should all genuine Christians. We must do all we can to stem the tide of marriage breakdown that is flooding our society, but the fact is that much as we oppose divorce, it happens – and occupies the time of many Christian workers and pastors. We therefore have a Christian responsibility to address the issue.

I have become concerned about the damage done by an inadequate understanding of what Scripture teaches about divorce. Tremendous spiritual and psychological pressure is exerted on innocent people in a marriage breakdown because of unsubstantiated church tradition and the pressure of family and friends. Innocent people caught up in the most horrible circumstances in their marriages become frustrated because they believe that divorce is always wrong. Many Christian men and women become the innocent victims in divorce actions because they have no clear guidelines. They bumble along and the resulting divorce or patched-up relationship is disastrous.

Clear, systematic guideline are necessary to clarify our thinking about divorce. For a victim who is being bullied, beaten, abandoned or cheated out of house, home, family or assets, the question arises: does the Bible have anything to say about this? I believe it does, and the answer to that question forms the gist of this book.

Hope for the Hurting

The following chapters offer hope to several categories of people who are affected by the devastation of marriage breakdown.

Firstly, there are those who have suffered a divorce. Their pain may be overwhelming and the emotional devastation may still be in progress.

Secondly, there are those facing a divorce that has not yet been finalised. If this is your position, you could be anywhere on the emotional scale: desperate to stop the divorce proceedings and try again, brokenhearted, despairing or even suicidal.

Thirdly, there are those who are not yet in the throes of divorce, but the conflict level in the relationship is so high that a divorce seems inevitable. You may panic at the prospect of losing everything and feel angry that this is happening to you.

Fourthly, there are those who have been divorced for some time but seem unable to free themselves from the past. They may even be the guilty ones whose irresponsible lives and unfaithful behaviour broke up their marriages. They are overwhelmed by regrets and anguish.

For all those experiencing marital breakdown, there is a way forward. It may not be possible to restore all that has been devastated, but you need not be trapped by misery, guilt and sadness. There is an escape route.

Hope starts with God. All the advice contained in this book begins with a right relationship with God. This may be a problem for some because they may feel that God has ignored their prayers and allowed their marriage to distintegrate; but whatever your perception may be, He is the sovereign ruler of the universe and to get perspective and a new foothold on life, we have to start with Him.

Heartache and hurt are the result of man's sinful nature. Our sinfulness has cut us off from God and in so doing it has severed us from the only Person who has the power to help us to make sense out of life. However, the good news is that Jesus opened the way to God through His death on the cross. As we come to Him, we find forgiveness and new life and strength. Christ transforms us and makes a new beginning possible. This must be our starting point.

Real hope for the hurting comes from the One who invented marriage. We need to know what He has to say about the marriage relationship, marriage breakdown and divorce. To the extent that we are willing to obey God's Word, there is hope.

A process of counselling, repentance and right action, based on the teachings of the Bible, opens the possibility for reconciliation and healing. This does not mean that your marriage will necessarily be saved, but if you are committed to right action, you will have a clean conscience before God and the knowledge that He will guide you.

To discard the myths and embrace God's truth about divorce is to begin a journey to freedom from unnecessary fear and emotional bondage. While it may be too late to save your marriage, freedom from guilt will enable you to build a new life in Christ.

The reader will notice that the greater part of this book is written from the woman's point of view. This is because, generally speaking, she is the injured party. However, I must stress that I am fully aware that the husband is not always responsible for the breakdown of a marriage. Women are sinners too and can be just as perverse as men. My personal counselling history is replete with examples of women who have broken up their marriages, abandoned their children, stolen the husbands of other women, lived recklessly and immorally and behaved destructively. The very incident of adultery presupposes the existence of a guilty woman. Whatever I have written by way of advice to the injured party therefore applies to both men and women. If you are the one who is hurting and having to deal with any of the situations or make any of the decisions suggested in these pages, this book is for you, whether you are a man or a woman.

As you read and reread these pages and think through the issues discussed in them, pray that God will break through your hurt to help you to understand what His Word has to say about your situation.

CHAPTER 1

Devastation

Some years ago I conducted a Sunday evening service on television. I took as my topic 'Six reasons why you should not get divorced.' The response was overwhelming. For a full twelve months I received letters and telephone calls, and people stopped me in the street and in shops to comment on what I had said. The sermon had touched an area of real need.

Some time later I published the sermon as a tract by the same title. We distributed it in the area around our church in preparation for a series of sermons on family living. A few days after we had handed out the tracts, I received one back in the mail. I have it before me now. Across the top an anonymous person had scrawled 'Six reasons why I *should*'. She had listed the following:

1. He knocks me about.
2. One of my children, aged 11, is in a psychiatric hospital because of the way his father molested him.
3. He earns R4,000 a month but gives me only R150 to feed and clothe *five* us (emphasis hers).

4. He sleeps around, with the result that he constantly has VD.
5. He only wants sex when he is drunk.
6. I hate him.

At the bottom of the page she had added: 'Frank, you live in a world that does not exist for most of the rest of mankind.'

How my heart went out to this woman! Little did she know just what my world consists of. Pastors sometimes deal with the dregs of humanity. We are often called upon to face, on a daily basis, some of the ugliest facets of life. I wanted to say to her: 'You should not be living like this! Why have you put up with the situation for so long? Have you sought help? If so, where? What did the counsellor say to you?'

I would have liked to explain to this woman that the Bible has a great deal more to say about divorce than the few ground rules I could offer in a ten-minute TV programme. While it is true that divorce was not part of God's plan for marriage and that we should avoid it if we can, it is equally true that the sort of abuse she had tolerated was also not part of God's plan for marriage.

Does the Bible have anything to say about this? What if one of the partners simply refuses to conduct the marriage by the rules? What if unfaithfulness, irresponsibility and abuse continue year in and year out? What if an uncaring partner simply does not care about the marriage any more, nor about the increasing emotional havoc he or she is causing in the lives of the children? What about the hurt, the dreadful shock and trauma of suddenly realising you are no longer loved or wanted? That's what we want to explore in this book.

People respond to the breakdown of a marriage in different ways. For some people it may be an exceedingly sordid and humiliating business while for others, especially when the divorce is by mutual agreement, it is dealt with in what is considered a cool and sophisticated manner. However, being cool and sophisticated about your marriage breaking up is not the common experience of most people.

Probably the majority of marriage problems we have dealt with involve sexual unfaithfulness and the alienation of the spouse's affection. This may sometimes be accompanied by abuse, but not always. Usually it is a shocking revelation to the betrayed spouse and being cool and sophisticated about it is highly unlikely. Take Cynthia for example.

Cynthia not only adored but admired her husband, Gary, a senior partner in a prominent firm. They lived in a well-to-do suburb and had three intelligent, healthy children. Church for Gary had become something to be tolerated rather than enjoyed as he climbed the ladder to financial success. Cynthia's carefully constructed life was shattered when she learned of Gary's affair. Emotionally, she fell apart. That was when I met her and became pastorally involved with the family.

Cynthia's life was in such disarray that trying to comfort her was like attempting to stop a waterfall. A talk to Gary did not help. He was used to negotiating big deals. A trained public relations man, he thought he could deal with me quite easily. He spoke quietly and reasonably about the impending divorce, with no sign of remorse except that he was sorry Cynthia was so upset. His arguments were garbled and made no sense, but like so many men caught up in an affair, he was mesmerised. He appeared to be listening, as he had been trained to do, but he was not. The meeting was a futile one.

Months of counselling followed, with support for Cynthia and the children. They wrote heartrending letters to their dad but all to no avail. His mind was made up. He wanted out. The emotional journey outlined in this chapter followed, with the added element of emotional cruelty.

Gary himself underwent all kinds of emotional changes. He swung from a hardened attitude to one of repentance and remorse. He allowed the events to drag on for three years – three long, emotionally devastating years in which he sent flowers, phoned and visited the family and dissolved into tears. He made promises, only to return to other women. The original affair was long over and other relationships had taken its place.

As so often happens, the longer reconciliation is delayed, the harder it becomes. From the caring father he had been, Gary's involvement with the family degenerated into heartlessness. Birthdays were forgotten. Dates with the children were not kept, and the children's anger grew at an alarming rate.

Shock, hurt, panic and confusion descended on Cynthia as the heart of the one she had spent so many happy years with, in the most intimate of relationships, seemed to turn to stone. In the years that followed, hope gave way to disappointment and finally the severing of all formal ties. Yet neither party was really free from the other because of the struggle of coping alone with the children continued, made more difficult by the realisation that the scars that had been inflicted on them would never disappear completely.

The one word that comes to mind to describe Cynthia's experience of conflict, confusion and pain is *devastation*. To devastate means to lay waste or make desolate, ravage or destroy. If this definition is accurate, it is a very apt description of divorce. Divorce devastates, and many a desolate heart will testify to the ravage and havoc of spirit and psyche, not to mention the loss of goods and assets so carefully accumulated over the years.

There are, in my opinion, at least four main areas of devastation brought about by a divorce.

Emotional devastation

First is *emotional devastation*. In some cases the trauma of divorce is like the death of a loved one. In fact, bereavement may be easier to bear. A divorce action has a tremendous emotional effect on the spouse who is left behind as well as on the children.

The emotional journey spirals down like this. The tremendous shock at the news that your spouse wants a divorce is followed by a period of denial. You refuse to believe that a third party is involved. Denial often engenders a powerful hope that it is all a nightmare, a terrible mistake. Your spouse will return – patience is all that is needed.

This leads to appeasement – attempts to win him or her back by arguing, reasoning, compliancy. You are willing to take the blame for the marriage break-up. You apologise profusely for your faults and promise to reform, even though you are the innocent party.

Panic, an increased sense of shock and a frantic search for help are the next stage. This develops into anger and retaliation, resentment and bitterness, accompanied by intense feelings of rejection, loss of self-worth and an unbelievable sense of loneliness. As a result, you may resort to uncharacteristic behaviour like one-night stands.

The final low is depression: a seemingly never-ending period of gloom, hopelessness and inexpressible sadness.

To add to this emotional battery, the guilty party often holds out hope to you: they may tell you that they do not want the divorce immediately, they just need time to think things through; they are confused and mixed-up; they really still love you, they just need time alone.

The journey may differ from person to person, especially if the marriage has been in trouble for years. The sequence may not always be the same but this, generally speaking, is the devastating emotional route a divorce action takes.

Social devastation
A second area of devastation is the *social* sphere. Divorce not only affects you and the children but a far wider circle of people. The grandparents are forced into an emotional crisis. Uncles and aunts on both sides of the family are affected. Friends, who do not want to take sides, are embarrassed and do not know how to relate to you. If you or your ex-spouse eventually remarries, a new set of grandparents, uncles and aunts further complicate social relationships.

Your ex-spouse's second marriage may be disturbed by an inability to break free from the influence of your relationship. Working out children's visiting days, if there is an unseen cauldron of bitterness, selfishness or jealousy, can cause a great deal of unpleasantness and hurt and result in tremendous rows week after week, with no opportunity for the high level of emotion to subside.

The distress of your children only adds to the unhappiness of the situation and spills over into your circle of anguished family and friends who watch the eruptions, unable to do anything about them. It seems that new relationships cannot be pursued unfettered. The social devastation never seems to end.

Economic devastation

Economic devastation is a third source of distress. Assets rightfully belonging to you may be claimed by your spouse, becoming a further source of acrimony and unpleasantness. After the divorce your standard of living may drop because the settlement and maintenance payments cannot support the lifestyle you enjoyed in marriage.

For a woman, job hunting and re-entering the marketplace may become a nightmare, administering a series of humiliating blows to your already low self-image.

If your ex-husband is unreliable, uncertain child support may be an area of ongoing conflict, especially if he remarries and has a new family to support.

Your ex-husband may, of course, be very conscientious about paying child maintenance. The problem may lie with you. Bitterness may cause you to seek revenge in petty ways, indulging in uncontrolled spending sprees, deliberately making extra expenses for him or constantly sending him lawyer's letters for increased support when you know he cannot meet these demands. This puts strain on him and adds to the economic and emotional devastation already being experienced.

Spiritual devastation

Most seriously of all, however, divorce can be *spiritually devastating* for the Christian. Caught up in one of life's most dreaded dramas, you are forced to draw on all available spiritual resources. You may often have had to comfort others in similar circumstances, but now you have to comfort yourself. Prayers to God for His intervention remain unanswered. God seems to be so far away that you wonder if He was ever there in the first place. Apart from everything else that has to be endured, there is a cascade of feelings of guilt, failure and shame, the suspicion that God has something against you, and the unanswered question: 'What have I done to deserve this?'

Added to this may be the feeling that the church disapproves of divorce and that, without understanding how, you have failed spiritually. You feel stigmatised, as if you can never be trusted again. Bitterness, hurt and resentment make you withdraw. You feel numb inside and, even though you may have been a committed Christian for many years, you act in uncharacteristic ways. You may hate yourself for this, but in your loneliness, instead of finding the spiritual help you always thought would be there, you may decide to have a fling.

No wonder the bottom line is: God hates divorce!

CHAPTER 2

Can my marriage be saved?

This is the heartrending question most people ask when they come to see us about marital problems. On the other hand, hurt and disillusioned people sometimes come to us with the opposite question: can I get out of this marriage?

Human sinfulness complicates our lives in such a way that marriage problems take on many different dimensions. It is not always easy to give quick and clear-cut answers to every situation. Sometimes a marriage dilemma has to be carefully thought through in the light of the Scriptures, and quiet, consistent application of the Scriptures needs to take place over a period of time.

A hurting spouse may ask the question 'Can I get a divorce?' when they really want an answer to the dilemma of getting an erring partner back again. Other people in pain may ask a question but not listen properly to the answer. They really want an opportunity to explain the problem, expressing their hurt and soliciting sympathy.

Irrespective of the complexity of the human heart, I have to say that with God's help, no one needs to get divorced. It is possible to save your marriage. However, that does not mean that your marriage *will* be saved.

That depends on a number of very important factors. These factors are discussed in the next chapter but a few preliminary comments may be helpful.

When your marriage cannot be saved

Your marriage stands very little hope of being salvaged if the problems causing the breakdown are not addressed.

How can any marriage continue with any form of integrity or dignity if, for instance, there is ongoing martial infidelity which your partner refuses to stop? Both people must want the marriage and be committed to it. Your partner is definitely not committed to you if he or she is seeing someone else. And if there is no willingness to change the situation, there really is no way forward.

The same applies if there is an unchanging pattern of abuse. How can a relationship exist if there is ongoing fear of physical or verbal assault? I will return briefly to this specific problem in chapter four and then look at it in more detail in chapter fourteen. But I want to stress that a marriage cannot be conducted with any form of viability if abuse is present.

Other factors that make it impossible for a marriage to be salvaged include the stress caused by bad habits such as gambling or drinking; financial stress brought about by irresponsibility and recklessness; an uncaring and inconsiderate attitude that causes a loss of self-worth and respect.

If things such as these are present and only one partner is willing to work at it, the situation is hopeless. There has to be a commitment from both partners if there is to be any hope for the future of their marriage.

I know this sounds pretty grim to people looking for a solution for their marriage problems, but unfortunately there are no easy remedies. Sometimes wives appeal to me to speak to their husbands, and vice versa. I am always willing to do so, but I know from years of experience that, with some exceptions, it is unlikely to bring any change. Marriage is a matter of commitment and if one party abandons that commitment, there is not much hope.

A case study

Some time ago a middle-aged couple came to see me. The visit was initiated by the husband who declared that he was anxious to save his marriage, while his wife showed no interest. They were sophisticated, upper middle-class people. He was a strong-willed, successful businessman, used to having his own way. She sat through the interview in reserved silence while he did all the talking.

He told how he had not always been the best of husbands; he had had his flings and made a few mistakes. But now he had reformed. When she informed him that she was no longer putting up with his behaviour, he suddenly realised that at their stage in life, a divorce would be very costly for him. He was now sure he wanted to keep his family intact – after all, they had been married for nearly thirty years.

For more than half an hour he dominated the conversation, giving her no opportunity to speak, nor asking for her comments. Finally I said to her, 'What's your side of the story?'

Tears filled her eyes as she told brokenly of years of lies, insults and infidelity. He looked increasingly more uncomfortable as she told me that even up to that moment, not much had changed. There was no sorrow or regret on his part, simply an arrogant magnanimity extended to her in that he was no longer going to see other women. All he wanted was for me to convince her to stay. After all, isn't that the teaching of the Bible?

Imagine his shock when I addressed them both. 'You,' I said to his wife, 'ought to leave my office and go to the nearest lawyer and start proceedings. This man is a liar and totally self-absorbed. There is no hope for this marriage while his attitude is unchanged.'

Turning to him, I said, 'You came in here and said you wanted straight talk. Here it is. You have manipulated and abused this woman for years. Now that it's going to cost you, you are manipulating her again. There is no way this marriage can be reconciled under these circumstances. I recommend that your wife leaves you as soon as possible.'

Deathly silence. His hands turned white as he gripped the arms of the chair, a look of utter disbelief on his face.

'Unless ...' I said, and paused. 'Unless you are willing to come to true repentance and a total surrender to Jesus Christ.'

They both looked at me a little bewildered. 'You see,' I continued, 'your life is full of bad habits accumulated over many years. You have mistreated your wife and children and you have no power to change yourself. But if you become a Christian and realise that the sins you committed offended not only your wife but Almighty God, then there is hope. There will still be a lot of work to do, but at least there is hope. Without that, there is no hope and I have nothing to offer you.'

A look of utter relief appeared on his wife's face. She knew what I was talking about. He was absolutely shocked at my brutal confrontation. He rose unsteadily to his feet, mumbled a greeting and left. I did not see them again and do not know how things turned out.

But do you see the point? How can a marriage work if there is no repentance and commitment? It does not matter who you see for advice. Many go to doctors and psychiatrists in a desperate search for help when their marriages disintegrate. But nothing will work if your partner does not want the marriage. Their problem is not medical or psychiatric; they have not left you because of a mental problem. They are doing what they are doing simply because they want to. Their problem is a spiritual one. They are defying God. They need to come to repentance. They need the power that only Christ can give to change.

When your marriage can be saved

A marriage can be saved if certain issues are faced squarely and truthfully. The most important question is this: do you really want each other? This is really the bottom line.

When I spoke to a couple recently about their problems, this question pulled them up. They were so focused on the difficulties, hurts and problems that had followed years of bickering and verbal sparring that they honestly felt there was no hope. I had to repeat this basic question several times before they really heard me. When they heard what I was saying, they began to think and both ultimately realised that they really did want each other.

I invite you to think about it. I know there may be a long history of hurt and disappointment, tension and conflict. But if your basic feeling about each other could be uncovered, would there be a desire to live in harmony and peace, love for each other and a desire to stay together? If you are angry and hurt, it's hard to answer this question because your reaction is likely to spring from your hurts. But keep mulling it over in your mind. Think about the arguments and bickering. Are they not mostly petty and of no real consequence?

We argue about silly things and allow our pride to get in the way. Everything is blown out of proportion. The distance between the two of you increases, and finally you stop speaking to each other. If someone had to ask you why you are not speaking to each other, you would probably not even remember the original reason. How utterly sad and inane.

An illustration

In 1993 my church suffered the horror of a terrorist attack during an evening service. This was during the build-up to the elections in South Africa when the political climate was volatile and terrorist attacks were one of the tactics used to keep the country in fear and instability. That traumatic evening saw eleven people killed and over fifty injured, some maimed for life.

The events and the lessons we learned are recorded in my book *Tragedy to Triumph*. But one lesson on which I want to comment again was the realisation of how short and uncertain life is. Young and old were killed that night, suddenly, unexpectedly and, of all places, in a church.

One couple had spent that weekend doing what so many couples do over weekends – arguing. They had exchanged words and were not speaking to each other. On the Sunday afternoon they kissed and made up. That night they came to church and he was killed by a terrorist bullet. Can you imagine the regrets if there had been no reconciliation?

We do not have that many weekends in one lifetime. What a waste to spend so many days of our short three-score-years-and-ten in silly and pointless conflict.

Let me put it to you another way. If you knew you were going to die in five minutes' time, what would matter to you? Would you care about who won the last argument? Would it matter who thinks what about you? Would all the little things that annoyed you so much in previous years really be so important if you knew that you would soon be facing God? Would you regret the language you have used, the insults you have heaped on your partner, the trauma you have caused your children? Most likely you would. It's a sobering experience to examine your life as if you were going to die in five minutes' time.

Your marriage can be saved if you both really want each other. If you both realise how utterly ridiculous it is to be controlled by petty and inconsequential things and are willing to abandon them, there is hope. Both of you must be determined to stop the ridiculous battle for one-upmanship in the home. You know what I mean – those verbal barbs and arrows, the repartee in an attempt to have the last word and to silence the other. What, ultimately is the point of it all?

What possible satisfaction can you get from hurting and humiliating the one you love? Not to mention the wounds you inflict on your children who watch the two of you in action.

Forgiveness brings hope

Forgiveness is an important subject that I will deal with again later, but I need to say that if you are willing to forgive your partner, your marriage can be saved. In plain terms, you have a choice. You can choose to live with bitterness and hurt or you can choose not to. If you choose to do so, what are the likely consequences?

The first is constant misery. You will focus on the offences committed against you. The more you dwell on them, the more you brood. Your mood becomes dark and self-centred. You think of yourself all the time. Self-pity sets in and you become a pain to live with.

I am not suggesting that you do not have cause to be hurt. Nor am I suggesting that the memories can be dispensed with easily. But if you have decided to keep the marriage going, it will not last if you live in the past. Your marriage can be saved if you are willing to face the past and deal with it once and for all. It may be your own past that needs to be dealt with, not your partner's. Whatever it is, it needs to be left behind.

There is only one way to deal sensibly with the past and that is to bring it to God. There we must seek forgiveness through our Lord Jesus Christ, leave the past and go forward. Your marriage can only be saved if you are willing to do that. If your partner has caused you a great deal of hurt but has truly repented, you must deal with the issues and accept your spouse again.

'But what if it happens again?' you may ask. Well, it might. There is no such thing as risk-free living. All relationships contain an element of risk. If you are a Christian, you have a great foundation on which to stand. If all the matters that have caused the problems have been dealt with as far as possible; if there has been repentance and a meaningful reconciliation, you should take the risk.

When the guilty partner is a Christian

Sometimes we are faced with the sad spectacle of Christians who are unable to deal with their problems and are facing divorce. This is indeed a great tragedy. Saying that it should not happen does not mean that it does not happen. It does, to everybody's great shame. It reflects badly on our Lord and Saviour and in fact negates the very gospel we preach. It has to be faced, dealt with and resolved.

Firstly, Christians should never see divorce as an option. They must seek help. To allow problems to accumulate to such a degree that a divorce is pending, is to admit that the Lordship of Jesus has been abandoned. Backsliding has taken place, self and carnality are ruling, and the devil has achieved a foothold in their lives.

However, although both partners are sometimes equally to blame, it is usually true that one of the partners is the guilty one while the other is struggling to hold things together. There is usually a great deal of anguish on the part of the innocent party. Their partner may have been a committed and involved member of the church community for many years, which leaves them confused and bewildered.

Sadly, we have to admit that Christians also succumb to the temptations of the world, the flesh and the devil. Therefore Christians have to be treated as anyone else would be. They need to be confronted and censured. If there is no repentance, they risk the possibility of losing their families and accruing the guilt of their hurt and hardship.

But another factor needs to be taken into account. It may well be that the erring partner may not be a true

Christian at all. Very often hurting wives tell me that their husbands have made 'a commitment to Christ'. But that commitment has not been followed by any real interest in Christian growth or activity. Occasional appearances in church are all that the commitment amounts to. They always make excuses about learning opportunities in the Christian faith. They show no real interest, yet when a problem occurs, the wife may say plaintively, 'But he is a Christian.'

The sad truth is that he may not be a Christian and is probably not regenerate or born again. We often have to explain to hurting spouses that, because their partners are not Christians, they cannot expect Christian behaviour from them. A person who is not a Christian cannot produce Christian behaviour, in spite of brief encounters with the church or Christian teaching.

This may be difficult for some to accept. They cling to the tenuous hope that, because they made a 'commitment', there is something higher to appeal to in them. For many of these erring partners, however, there is no real spiritual interest to which we can appeal. Whatever spiritual experience they may have had, it was not the new birth that gives us a new nature with spiritual motivation and instinct.

Can my marriage be saved?
I wish I could say with certainty that your marriage *will* be salvaged. To my great regret, that is not possible. However, assuming that your spouse is willing to be reconciled to you, I want to say that your marriage *can* be saved.

Often the betrayed or hurt partner is caught in the

grip of anger and deep hurt which may harden the heart against the possibility of a reconciliation. I will talk about the possibility and impossibility of reconciliation in chapters four and five. At this point I want to examine the relevant Scriptures and stress the desirability of reconciliation as the Christian option.

CHAPTER 3

Reconciliation –
What does the Bible say?

Three key passages clarify the biblical principles that should guide our thinking on the process of reconciliation between two people in a marriage relationship. These are Matthew 5:23-26, Matthew 18:15-17 and 1 Corinthians 7:10-16. We will look at each in some detail.

Matthew 5:23-26

Matthew 5:23-26 forms part of the Sermon on the Mount. It sketches two scenes, one dealing with offerings and altars, i.e. an act of worship, the other with settling disagreements, courts and judges, i.e. a civil and legal matter.

Our Lord is saying that, whether it be in our spiritual life or civil and legal concerns, broken relationships affect us. We are exhorted to go and be reconciled, and to settle matters quickly.

A reconciliation between marriage partners is particularly desirable for two reasons. Firstly, it is the godly thing to do. Before we can come into God's presence to worship Him, we have to ensure that the broken relationship with our brother is healed. God deals with us on the basis of our reconciliation with Him in Christ.

Reconciled relationships between Christians therefore reflect the reality of our spiritual life.

Secondly, it is the prudent thing to do. In Jesus' day a failure to settle matters quickly had very uncomfortable consequences indeed – you could be thrown into prison.

Bearing these two principles in mind, think of the ongoing, complicated consequences of a divorce. It is far better to take the godly and prudent reconciliation route.

Matthew 18:15-17

Matthew 18:15-17 presents both the desirability of reconciliation and the 'how to'. The procedure is illustrated for us in a case study.

A believer sins against his brother. He is reluctant to be reconciled, but the other is anxious to do so. Notice, as a matter of interest, that in the Matthew 5 passage your brother has something against you, while in the Matthew 18 passage you have something against him. It therefore makes no difference who is responsible for the problem or who is the offended party. As a believer, the onus is on you to start the reconciliation process. Four steps are outlined.

Step 1 is a private confrontation between the two parties.

Step 2 includes one or two arbitrators in an attempt to ensure fairness and reconciliation.

Step 3 includes the church or, if you like, the highest court of appeal that you can turn to in your Christian circle for help in reconciliation, particularly if both parties are believers.

Step 4 involves the discipline of the unrepentant party by treating him as an unbeliever and cutting him off from the fellowship and privileges of the people of God.

Although this passage is presented as a problem between

'brothers', the dynamics given by Jesus are relevant to all relationships. Thus this process is very relevant to those facing the possibility of marriage breakdown. Step 1 is tried, perhaps without much success. The failure may be due to circumstances, making it almost impossible to talk without emotions gaining the upper hand. Step 2 entails calling in family, friends or the church to help. If this fails, Step 3 follows. This involves using the biggest guns you have, and may take the form of a lawyer's letter if your spouse is not interested in church opinion. If these three steps meet with no response, the final step is taken. A cut-off point is reached in Step 4.

The assumption is that both parties are believers, but the same principles apply even if one of them is not. These are universal principles of common sense. Confrontation, reasoning and counsel form part of the reconciliation process but if these fail, a cut-off point is finally reached.

It is important to notice that the New Testament teaches that a limit may be reached in the reconciliation process. So often well-meaning Christians counsel others to go on praying and hoping, cajoling, scolding and pleading, and the matter drags on interminably, increasing hatred and resentment.

1 Corinthians 7:10-16

In this passage Paul deals with the situation where one spouse has become a Christian and the other has not. The Christian spouse should attempt to hold the marriage together as far as it lies in his or her power to do so. Let us examine the principles that emerge from it.

Firstly, if a separation does occur, *the Christian is to remain unmarried* (v. 11) so that he or she does not enter another relationship on the rebound. An unseemly and hasty remarriage must be avoided. Time must be given to cool off and there must be an opportunity for reconciliation to be effected.

It is interesting to note that, while both wife and husband are commanded not to leave their spouse (vv. 10-11), Paul adds: 'But if she does ...' the wife is granted permission to be an exception to the rule, presumably because she is usually the one in danger of being physically hurt. Most husbands do not need physical protection from their wives!

Secondly, *if an unbelieving spouse is willing to live with the believing spouse, there must be no separation or divorce.* The fact that the spouse is unconverted does not provide grounds for a divorce.

Notice the word 'willing to live with' (vv. 12-13). This implies that the unbelieving spouse is willing to make life normal and bearable for the Christian because he is prepared to live with her as a believer. If he says he wants the marriage to continue but then places demands on the believer that are in direct opposition to her faith, causing tension and conflict, he is indicating that he is *not* 'willing to live with' her.

Thirdly, *if the unbeliever wishes for a separation, it should be granted* (v. 15). We assume that Paul meant that the unbeliever may not be prepared to live with a Christian. He may forsake all sense of tenderness and partnership with the Christian and create a situation in the home that makes a normal family life impossible. The action of the unbeliever may indicate patently that he has rejected his Christian spouse even though he may not immediately leave the home. Paul says, 'it should be granted'. In other words, allow the relationship to end.

There must be a cut-off point. God has called us to live in peace (v. 15). A life that is constantly filled with tension, ugliness and conflict is contrary to God's will for His people. It mitigates against their spiritual progress and is inappropriate as a Christian witness.

Fourthly, '*a brother or sister is not under bondage in such cases*' (v. 15, NKJV). This seems to refer to the command of the Lord quoted in verses 10 and 11 which lays down the general rule that a wife must not separate from her husband and a husband must not divorce his wife. Certain circumstances may develop within the marriage where the Christian, who would normally be bound to an unbelieving spouse, is no longer bound.

Paul seems to be saying that it is not God's will to be trapped for ever in a situation of hopeless marital misery. If your partner, by his actions, places no value on the marriage, let the marriage cease. You are no longer bound to the relationship. You are permitted, by a great redeeming God to be freed from the misery of being the victim of another's sinful behaviour. This freedom must include permission to remarry, for the Bible does not teach the possibility of divorce without the possibility of remarriage.

This passage therefore teaches that a marriage partner who becomes a Christian and lives with an unsaved spouse faces two alternatives. Either the non-Christian spouse is willing to live with the Christian spouse in such a way that they accept the Christian spouse's beliefs and make life bearable for them. If this is the case, the Christian must work towards reconciliation. If the reconciliation process fails and divorce becomes inevitable, the Christian must not remarry for a time, to allow for the possibility of reconciliation. If this proves to be impossible, the objecting spouse must be released from his or her commitment to the marriage and leave the believing partner to live in peace.

Summary

All this may sound very technical and perhaps a little cold, but it is important that this process is clearly understood. In the confusion of marriage breakdown, people need guiding principles.

The first priority is always reconciliation. Initiatives do not always succeed but, for the Christian, they must be taken. Have you tried this? Or have you withdrawn into bitterness and resentment in such a way that you are closing the door on this option?

To summarise, we should work for reconciliation for the following reasons:

1. It is the godly thing to do.

2. It is the prudent thing to do.

3. There is a procedure to be followed, that involves calling in help on different levels.

4. There is a cut-off point.

5. If such a cut-off point is reached, it does not leave the innocent party chained to singleness and loneliness for the rest of their life. It releases them from a life of tension and misery and frees them to marry again.

6. The guiding principle for the believer is that God has called us to live in peace. This does not refer to the normal tensions of married life with another human being as fallen and sinful as yourself. Rather, it refers to ongoing marital strife and conflict. There must be peace and harmony for you to be a witness to others.

CHAPTER 4

When reconciliation is possible

Continued bad behaviour and unresolved marriage difficulties make reconciliation between warring spouses impossible in the long run. Christian principles and common sense make such a compromise undesirable. Yet it is possible, with God's help, to create conditions under which real, meaningful reconciliation becomes possible.

While there are no guarantees, a marriage partner can take certain steps to facilitate this process, creating an atmosphere in which discussion and counselling can take place.

Such a climate may be created by five lines of action: censure unacceptable behaviour; make conditions for reconciliation; allow time apart for reflection, repentance and change; pray for reconciliation, and do what is right. Unceasing prayer to the God and Father of our Lord Jesus Christ should undergird everything.

1. Censure unacceptable behaviour
Gary Richmond, in his book entitled *The Divorce Decision*, mentions three things that are always unacceptable. These are the three As – abuse, adultery and abandonment.

These three words cover a multitude of actions. Abuse

is not necessarily physical. It may be vile, demaning, verbal insults. I am not talking about the insults and bad language that may sometimes be used in a burst of temper, harmful as that is, but about the language of ongoing strife, tension and conflict. It could include talk that undermines your self-confidence, negates you as a person of worth or wears you down psychologically. A Christian should refuse to accept this. This is not the purpose of marriage.

The marriage vows in our church are preceded by the following words:

> *Minister* (to the Bridegroom): John, will you have this woman, Mary, to be your wedded wife, to live together according to God's commands in the holy relationship of marriage? Will you love her, comfort her, honour and keep her, in sickness and in health; and forsaking all others, keep yourself only for her, so long as you both live?

> *Bridegroom*: I will.

> *Minister* (to the Bride): Mary, will you have this man, John, to be your wedded husband, to live together according to God's commands in the holy relationship of marriage? Will you obey him, serve him, love, honour and keep him, in sickness and in health; and forsaking all others, keep yourself only for him, so long as you both live?

> *Bride*: I will

These words of intent precede the marriage vows. They contain the promises about the future treatment the couple may expect from each other. This declaration of intent is couched in words that are meaningful and the entire flow of the service is one of tenderness, respect and commitment.

Breaking your marriage vows is therefore not limited to an adulterous relationship. You break your vows when you reject the partner you promised to have and to hold, to love, comfort and honour. As long as a marriage partner is allowed to get away with disrespect, he or she will never be truly reconciled to you. Respect must be demanded.

Some people believe that everything will automatically 'come right' if they quietly do all the right things such as not answering back and not provoking their partner. Of course demeaning yourself by entering a slanging match is unacceptable, but allowing abuse to continue unabated will destroy your self-respect. Your children will learn that this kind of behaviour is acceptable in marriage. Your children should observe you taking marriage so seriously that you refuse to put up with abusive behaviour.

Ongoing abuse of a wife by her husband makes reconciliation impossible. But conversely, when it dawns on your spouse that you will not put up with such behaviour, you gain new dignity in his eyes. A sense of shame may well develop in him. By drawing the boundary lines, you demonstrate that if he continues to overstep the mark, he will lose you.

The same principle applies to adultery and permissiveness. A Christian should refuse to accept this. If you are contemplating a reconciliation but suspect that your spouse is playing the field, postpone it. If he has not learned his lesson and is not serious about negotiating with you, he is a liar and a deceiver.

Ray Sutton makes a suggestion in his book *Second*

Chance that warrants serious consideration. When an unfaithful partner wants reconciliation and this is arrived at, the party who has been sinned against should demand a clean bill of health first.

A Christian should also refuse to accept the irresponsible behaviour of an unpredictable spouse that could be described as abandonment. Drinking parties, absences for a night or two and holidays by himself are definitely unacceptable. A husband's place is at home with his family, who should be his first concern. If he insists on living like a bachelor, do not be fooled. A wife is meant to be more than a housekeeper, launderer, cook and sex partner. The same rules apply of course to a wife who behaves irresponsibly.

Take a stand on abuse, adultery or abandonment. Defining clearly the ground rules for reconciliation will command respect. Discussion and counselling can now take place at a serious and intelligent level, creating the right climate for true reconciliation.

Love for your spouse, as James Dobson says, must be tough. Allowing your husband's sinful attitudes to continue in the hope of getting him back and keeping your family together will not work, as thousands of unhappy women can testify.

2. Make conditions

People are sometimes surprised when I suggest that it is necessary to make conditions for reconciliation, but I believe that it is essential. So many partners, especially women, give in to sweet talk. There may be such a longing for the marriage to work that the hurting partner is tempted to believe almost anything and returns to the family home without any of the problems having been resolved.

There is no point in going back to a situation from which you have withdrawn if the situation and your spouse have not changed. The longing and the vague, unsubstantiated hope that he or she will change is not enough. Real reconciliation is only possible if you insist on a repentance of wrong acts, an agreement to change the habits that caused the marriage to break down, and a willingness to seek counselling help.

Many men resist this notion. Pride makes them believe that they can resolve their own problems. There is also, understandably, a measure of embarrassment at the thought of discussing marital problems with a third party, but the innocent partner should insist on repentance and counselling.

I have been asked whether forgiveness should not be unconditional and whether the two people should not be encouraged to get together at the earliest opportunity. While *forgiveness* may be extended unconditionally, reconciliation cannot be. To forgive somebody for doing you an injury is one thing. Deliberately placing yourself in a position where the unrepentant party could continue to hurt you is quite another.

I wonder whether forgiveness is, in fact, totally unconditional. In the Lord's Prayer, we ask for forgiveness from God, adding the assurance that we forgive those who sin against us. Our Lord assures us that if we do not forgive others, we will not be forgiven (Matt. 6:14-15). In other words, receiving forgiveness must have concomitant consequences in our lives.

The parable in Matthew 18:21-35 illustrates this

point. The man who owed his master a lot of money was freely and totally forgiven, but there was an implied responsibility on him to act in accordance with his newly received forgiveness. When he refused to forgive someone who owed him a relatively small sum of money, he was judged.

The grace and forgiveness of God are large and free. They cannot be earned or merited. But is forgiveness unconditional? Are repentance and faith not required? These principles apply to the relationship with an erring spouse. It is vital that you lay down clear conditions, make plain that these must be met and challenge unacceptable behaviour in your partner. If this has never been done seriously before, do it now. Lay down the conditions for a real and lasting reconciliation.

3. Time out

As a woman, if you have separated pending a divorce because of the bad behaviour of your spouse, there must be time for him to reflect on what life is like without you. Several important lessons are learned during this painful time. Let us look at some of them.

The erring spouse learns what it is like to live without the love, warmth and comfort of a faithful partner. Coming home to an untidy house, dirty shirts, cold rooms, an empty freezer and silence provides the opportunity for him to assess how he really feels about you. If he can cope without you and does not really want you except for the bedroom comforts you provide, the sooner you know this, the better. If he really loves you, time away from you will increase his distress and desperation and prepare the ground for a meaningful, conditional reconciliation.

Time apart creates the opportunity for the guilty party to reflect on the wrong behaviour that caused the marriage to break down and to prove whether there has been genuine repentance or not. A change of mind about past wrong behaviour and a corresponding change of attitude and action constitutes more than words and promises. It must be seen. Time is needed for him to seek help and to change his ways. Men do change for a while to get their wives back. It is therefore important that the erring spouse establishes his spiritual and behavioural bona fides.

Time should be given for respect and trust to develop again. The loss of respect is the most destructive influence on any relationship. After years of abuse, adultery or abandonment and treating the marriage partner as though she were useless, the guilty partner needs to learn that his spouse is a person with worthy and dignity. He must realise that if he does not respect and want her, it is quite possible that someone else will. He must discover once again that she is a desirable person. He will not learn that if she makes herself too readily available. He must also learn that he cannot have this desirable person unless he respects her. A period of aloofness is needed to establish the climate for reconciliation.

Marriage partners do not own each other, yet it is amazing how many couples view each other as their property. Marriage should be a partnership that helps both husband and wife to grow because each is concerned about serving the other and caring for his or her well-being. It should be a life-long commitment to their partner, prepared for them by God. They have no right to impact on each other's lives in such a way that their spiritual development is stunted.

1 Corinthians 6:19-20 (NKJV) reads:

> Or do you not know that your body is the temple of the Holy Spirit who is in you, whom you have from God, and you are not your own? For you were bought at a price; therefore glorify God in your body and in your spirit, which are God's.

Christians are owned by God, created by Him and purchased by His Son's blood on the cross. There can be no oppressive 'ownership' of the other that causes one partner to believe that they can say and do as they please. When this is understood, reconciliation is made easier. A time apart during a divorce action where a reconciliation is desired helps to establish this principle.

A time apart and the refusal to enter too hastily into a reconciliation gives the innocent partner the opportunity to make sure that all subsidiary problems have been faced and an honest attempt has been made to deal with them. If there has been a drinking problem or a problem with substance abuse, the partner should receive help. If there has been an attitudinal problem, he or she should seek counsel. If there has been a problem with infidelity, this has to be set aside firmly and finally.

The extent to which these and a host of other difficulties that destroy marriages are being dealt with can be assessed if the guilty spouse is allowed time out. Do not rush back. Sometimes the guilty spouse will put great pressure on the other to return, making all kinds of promises and probably pushing all the right emotional buttons. But, I repeat, do not be in a hurry to go back.

I fully understand the emotional upheaval on everybody involved when a couple separates. One of the pressure points is the children. Often they are desperate to get their parents together. And equally often you realise only too well that they need both parents' input. On the other hand I have known plenty of instances when children dread a father going back or, for that matter, a mother. Women are just as perverse as men and are often guilty of destroying the home. I have personally seen a number of instances where the mother is no longer welcome in the home. Depending on what has happened in the relationship, children may not want the erring parent to be part of their lives again.

Be careful of pressure. Painful though it may be, you must resist the pressure to return too soon. Some books and marriage counsellors recommend that the partners should get together as soon as possible, but let us remember Paul's words in 1 Corinthians 7:10-11 (NKJV):

> Now to the married I command, yet not I but the Lord: a wife is not to depart from her husband. But even if she does depart, let her remain unmarried or be reconciled to her husband. And a husband is not to divorce his wife.

The ideal is for a couple to remain together, but if they separate, the Christian partner must not remarry too soon to give them time to work at reconciliation. Time apart encourages reflection and reassessment and may help to create a climate in which reconciliation becomes possible.

4. Prayer
Do you believe in prayer? True Christians who have been born again may come to God with confidence. They and they alone have the right to call Him Father. Why do

I say that? Because it is sadly possible to think you are a Christian when in fact you are not. You may be good, decent, upright, even churchgoing. Yet for all that you may not know Christ personally. Do you know Him?

Knowing Christ and having a sure and certain relationship with God through Him does not necessarily solve all your problems. But it does place your feet on a rock that is steadfast and sure when everything else is shaking. What's more, you have access into His presence and can enjoy the confidence of knowing that your prayers are being heard.

On one occasion our Lord responded to the request of His disciples and taught them about prayer (Luke 11:1-13). He said: 'When you pray, say: Our Father ...' The Aramaic word for father, *Abba*, conveys the greatest possible intimacy between a father and a son. The Jews used the more formal word *Abihu* when approaching God, but Jesus used the word that implies intimacy, spontaneity and privilege – *Abba*.

Jesus used this word in Gethsemane when He wrestled with the prospect of the cross (Mark 14:36). Paul uses it in Romans 8:15 and Galatians 4:6 to indicate something of the enormous privilege of the unique relationship a Christian has with God. He is *our* Father. What a glorious name!

The Lord's Prayer teaches us several important things about coming to our *Abba* in heaven. Jesus said that we may ask Him for our daily bread (Luke 11:3). Bread is used as a figure of speech to cover all our earthly needs. A house, family and restored relationship are also daily needs. Under the umbrella of 'our daily bread', we may come to *Abba* to implore Him to change hard hearts, bring true repentance and create an atmosphere in which real reconciliation which will honour Him can take place.

Jesus also taught us to persist in prayer. He said that if we keep on asking, seeking and knocking, it would be given us, we would find, and the door would be opened (vv. 9-10). What an assurance! He instructed us to remember what our Father is like. We are evil, yet we know how to do good to our children. God is good. How much more then will He not give the Holy Spirit to them who ask (vv. 11-13).

Luke 18:1 (NKJV) says:

> Then He spoke a parable to them, that men always ought to pray and not lose heart.

This is God's will for those who are facing the strain and tension of separation and possible reconciliation. *Always* pray, do not give up. I cannot promise that your desires will be granted because God's purposes and ways are often hidden from us. But He hears our prayers and will always act on behalf of those who truly belong to Him. He may seem not to have your welfare or that of your children at heart at the time of hurt and separation, but He has.

Whatever happens, do not be tempted to believe that He has lost control of your life. Pray and entrust yourself to Him who turns the hearts of men as He wills. If you are His child, he is your *Abba*, Father. His arms are strong, His power immense, His will unshakeable and His love immeasurable.

Prayer is an indispensable tool for reconciliation. You may not have the wisdom to meet the need of the occasion. Your insights, judgements and assessments may be limited and finite, but His are not. As you pray, He makes reconciliation and change possible.

5. Do what is right

It may be very difficult to do what is right. Very often the level of anger and resentment during a separation or divorce is so high that you fervently hope you will never be called on to go back to the marriage. However, all things being equal and all conditions being met, your responsibility is to do what is right.

I often hear people say: 'But I do not love him any more'. That, for the Christian, is not the sole criterion. A Christian seeks to live by biblical principles and to work for the welfare of the other. The expressions of love can be learned again and will be restored if you obey, because God honours faithfulness to His Word.

On the other hand, doing what is right may mean *not* going back to the marriage when every part of you desperately wants to do so. You may be tempted to short-circuit the entire reconciliation process and place yourself and your children again in an ungodly situation of chaos and conflict. To do what is right may entail going through with the divorce. Some wives are willing to do everything we advise them to do except this last thing.

If your spouse detects that you mean business and are willing to do what is right, there is often a subtle change of attitude and the climate for reconciliation is created. Whatever it entails – apologising, confessing sin, admitting to your share in the marriage breakdown, accepting your partner's proven bona fides or being willing to go through with the divorce – if you genuinely want reconciliation, as a Christian you are under an obligation to be ready, willing and prepared to do what is right.

We need to realise, however, that there are conditions under which reconciliation is impossible. We will examine these in the following chapter.

CHAPTER 5

When reconciliation is impossible

Attempts at reconciliation may fail. A person responsible for the breakdown of his or her marriage may be confronted and counselled at length, urged, reasoned with and reproved, yet obstinately refuse to budge. Proverbs 29:1 says:

> A man who remains stiff-necked after many rebukes,
> will suddenly be destroyed – without remedy.

In Matthew 18:15-17 our Lord teaches us that when a believer refuses to be reconciled with his brother, he is finally cut off from the privileges of the believing community. He is, as it were, 'divorced' from the church.

It is vitally important for all who face marital difficulties to realise that there may come a time when they have to accept that attempts at reconciliation have failed. It is therefore important to understand the conditions under which reconciliation is impossible. Many people, desperate to save their marriages, have sought reconciliation and been overhasty to believe that the erring partner is willing to work at it, only to have their hopes shattered. They allow the heartache and devastation to continue indefinitely.

s look at ten conditions under which genuine ation between two people is impossible. Heeding these and resisting the overwhelming temptation to overlook them, in the blind hope that things will somehow work out, will avoid a great deal of heartache.

1. Refusal to communicate

It is amazing how many wives make excuses for their husbands' refusal to communicate and how many men excuse themselves on the grounds that 'I am the quiet type', 'I find it difficult to express myself'. Lack of communication is one of the leading factors in marriage breakdown.

As a rule, women communicate far more easily than men do. They need to talk and express their feelings. Men generally find it more difficult to show their emotions. Some never convey any response – positive or negative – to their wives or children. While men may find it more difficult to communicate, this must never become an excuse for not doing so. It is imperative to talk, especially when the marriage relationship is already strained. A refusal to engage in discussion, reasoning and meaningful argument about the situation in the home, effectively closes the door to reconciliation.

God is a Trinity and there is always happy, harmonious communication in the relationships between the Father, the Son and the Holy Spirit. God has created us so that the primary and most important way to resolve problems is by talking. This is part of what it means to be created in His image. He has created us to function in relationship to others, and primarily to our marriage partners. To refuse to verbalise our thoughts and feelings is therefore not only a denial of the image of God in us, with all the spiritual implications that has, but a refusal to face up to the problem.

I strongly urge any who are faced with the possibility of reconciliation, without meaningful dialogue regarding the problems that caused the marriage to break down, to resist coming together in this way. Problems do not disappear automatically. They will resurface. Ignoring them is merely postponing the evil day. Insist on talking, preferably with the help of an experienced counsellor. Without talking, true reconciliation is impossible.

In this regard it may be helpful to warn those who are considering marriage, especially women, to watch for this trait in their intended spouse. If he is not communicating meaningfully with you now, it will only get worse as the years go by. If he tends to lapse into long periods of silence, you should pick up the warning signs. Insist that he gets help to change or seriously rethink your relationship. This may sound extreme, but picture the relationship in twenty years' time! Thinking the issue through now could avoid a great deal of unhappiness in the future.

Real communication requires discipline, will-power and practice. As Christians we need to understand the importance of expressing the image of God in our relationships with others. No communication means no reconciliation. At best, this kind of reconciliation will be a patch-up job that is unlikely to last.

2. Loss of respect

Some years ago, a friend remarked to me that we could never be friends if we ceased to respect each other. I have never forgotten those words. They are as pertinent to marriage relationships as to friendships.

Many married couples live for years in the most demeaning circumstances. They tolerate insults and abuse, not realising that they are undermining their own self-respect as well as the respect of their partner. The situation is aggravated when, in fits of temper, they hurl abuse at each other. I am referring here primarily to verbal abuse. I will deal with physical abuse later.

Respect cannot exist in an atmosphere of abuse. As a woman, the more you allow yourself to be insulted, the more you increase your own sense of hurt and humiliation. Years of abuse cannot be eradicated overnight. If your spouse requests a reconciliation, refuse it. An abusive partner needs a fairly long period of time to prove himself and to establish his bona fides.

No one has the right to abuse another. When one spouse refuses to acknowledge the other as a worthy human being, all respect has gone and, with it, the opportunity for reconciliation. No reconciliation can take place unless there is respect, and respect cannot exist in an atmosphere of abuse.

The same applies to a spouse who refuses to behave as a worthy human being. Lies, sexual perversion and marital unfaithfulness undermine respect and dignity. Even such seemingly small things such as body odour, dress and house-keeping can cause conflict and tension. I am not suggesting perfection. Rather, I am trying to underscore this vital ingredient of respect for all healthy relationships. As it is necessary for you to be respected, it is also necessary for you to respect your partner. If your partner behaves in such a way that you and your children are continually filled with disgust, no lasting reconciliation is possible.

Many well-meaning wives return to a husband who has not resolved his drinking problem. They believe, mistakenly, that a temporary separation has taught him a lesson. They soon discover that he has learned nothing. Feelings of pity are not a genuine basis for reconciliation.

Second Samuel 6:16-23 is a classic case of God's judgement on a woman who lost respect for her marriage partner. Admittedly, this is not a usual marriage dispute and the history of both David and Michal was complicated, but the principle is clear. Michal despised her husband for dancing before the Lord in what she considered an undignified manner. Her disrespect manifested itself in cutting remarks. The last reference we have to her in the Bible are the words: 'And Michal daughter of Saul had no children to the day of her death' (v. 23). Whatever else this may mean, it indicates God's displeasure.

I want to urge all who are seeking reconciliation with their marriage partner in an atmosphere of insult, diatribe, accusation and disrespect to think again. There can be no lasting reconciliation where there is no respect.

3. Fear

Fear can be present for numerous reasons, the most common being violence and abuse. A violent home is a fearful home. Who has not heard of women scared almost out of their wits by the violent actions of their husbands? We have become all too familiar with stories of blackened eyes, broken noses and ribs, and the sickening thud of fist on flesh.

I do believe that a Christian woman has the right to remain in such a situation yet, amazingly, many women are loathe to leave and live in hope that things will improve. Some believe that it is their Christian duty to submit to this treatment because their husband is 'the head of the house' and their marriage vows are important.

This is a distortion of an important truth concerning family relationships and the roles the partners should be playing. It is true that God has made the man the head of the home, but there are other laws of God that are equally important.

The world does not use headship in a biblical sense but rather to define who is the boss. Unfortunately many Christians have adopted this view. Headship, as intended by God, is described in 1 Corinthians 11:3:

> Now I want you to realise that the head of every man is Christ, and the head of every woman is man, and the head of Christ is God.

The biblical view of the headship of the man to the woman is defined in terms of the relationship that Christ has to man and God has to Christ. Let us think about that for a moment. How does Christ relate to us? And how does God relate to Christ?

Christ has taken upon Himself the obligation to be our Saviour and Redeemer. As a result of this relationship with us, He takes the initiative to care for and protect us. True headship therefore includes the responsibility to think about and take the initiative in advancing the true well-being of the other person in the relationship. Just as we have a responsibility to respond to Christ by loving Him and obeying His laws, so the wife responds to her husband who acts as a true head – not a bossy, unbiblical tyrant – and seeks to advance her husband's interests. Any other notion of headship is unbiblical.

A Christian man who practises his headship in a dictatorial and domineering way is acting sinfully. Any man who is more concerned about himself and his own status in the family than those for whom he should be caring is failing in his task. God never intended marriage and the home to be filled with fear and violence. The role of headship is not one of ownership and superiority but of friendship and equality.

However, fear can be present even though there is no overt violence. Where there is fear, violence or a threat of violence, geninue reconciliation is impossible. But violence is not the only cause of fear in marriage.

Many wives feel unable to recommit themselves to their husbands because of financial instability or recklessness. A man who cannot manage money properly and keeps his family in debt, depriving them of what is rightfully theirs, causes great anxiety and stress. It is not only the big debts that cause problems. Little things such as unpaid school fees, new shoes that cannot be afforded or a small birthday present unbought cause stress. It is not possible to live with this for any length of time, and if these things are not dealt with, there can be no meaningful reconciliation. I am not referring here to the genuine hardships that many people encounter, but rather hardships that are the result of recklessness.

Financial irresponsibility sometimes goes hand in hand with frequent changes of job and home. Again, I am not referring to the normal stresses families endure in the attempt to make ends meet in an inflation-laden society. Nor am I referring to the changes of job and dwelling that may occasionally be involved as better job opportunities occur.

I am referring here to an irresponsibility that constantly places the family under strain and makes them uncertain what the next move will be because the breadwinner is reckless and unpredictable and the partner has to provide for the family.

The fear brought about by financial and personal irresponsibility is just as ruinous to reconciliation as physical or verbal abuse. This kind of insecurity and fear makes it impossible for a true reconciliation to take place.

If you find yourself in this situation, please be careful. Do not be persuaded to reconcile on the basis of unproven promises. Have you heard these promises before? How many times have you tried a reconciliation on this basis, only to be hurt again? You cannot undertake a reconciliation on trust alone. Trust is important in any reconciliation, but trust has to be earned and proven, not merely professed. 'Trust me, I mean business this time' is a hollow promise.

4. Unresolved problems

Whatever the causes of marriage breakdown, they need to be examined and resolved. Sometimes the heart so longs for the loved one that, in a moment of panic or regret, all the problems and reasons for separation are momentarily pushed aside. In a surge of hope a reconciliation is effected, with the desperate longing that it will work out somehow. Unfortunately there is not much in life that works out 'somehow'. Problems have to be faced and dealt with for reconciliation to have a chance.

If, for instance, your partner has had a series of adulterous relationship and you have withdrawn from the relationship pending a divorce, there is no point in going back if his or her lifestyle has not changed. If there is no repentance of and departure from unfaithfulness, abuse, gambling, drinking or whatever the particular problem is, there is no possibility of a genuine reconciliation.

Two problems are especially common in marriage breakdown. The one is alcoholism and the other is physical abuse. They often go hand in hand. I want to state quite categorically that unless these problems have been faced and resolved, true reconciliation is impossible. The relationship may be temporarily patched up and things may go well for a while, but these problems are so serious that unless they have been rooted out, they will recur. Alcoholics must agree to a drying-out process and serious counselling. If you are being physically abused, you need to be very firm.

Emerson and Russell Dobash, the authors of *Violence Against Wives*, make the point that women often leave a violent home temporarily without intending this act to be permanent. There may be a number of reasons for this. Their husbands make promises that convince them; they believe that their leaving has taught him a lesson; they feel that they have the ability to change him and make the marriage work; some believe it is their duty to keep the marriage together. I want to say as firmly as I am able to that it is *wrong* to stay in a situation of this nature. There can be no reconciliation worthy of the name until this problem has been resolved.

A great unresearched social phenomenon is a woman's faithfulness to her partner. Of course it is not always so, because women are sinners too and are often the cause of the heartache in the home. But generally speaking, women offer a great deal of support to their husbands even though they may have been abused or betrayed. They endure much hurt in the hope that the situation will change. They often accept their husbands' hollow promises that they will change because they so desperately want their homes to remain intact.

A point must be reached when these empty promises are recognised for what they are. There must be a refusal to be persuaded and an insistence on real change, with adequate time being given for this change to be expressed. Without this, there can be no reconciliation. More about this in chapter fourteen.

5. Lack of commitment

Many people think that commitment is something that just happens. They may say, 'I'll stick it out, no matter what'. This is not really thinking at all. True commitment is an intellectual decision made on the basis of specific information. For instance, your partner says that he or she loves you, will provide/care for you and be faithful to you. While some people do choose their marriage partner in an emotional way, with the resultant problems, most people make their commitment with the firm conviction that they will be true to the marriage.

If you marry someone you know will not be faithful to you, the decision is not an intellectual but an emotional one. A serious commitment looks at all the facts, recognises possible difficulties, and enters the marriage determined to work positively and intelligently for its success.

Having made a reasoned decision to get married, one of the partners may begin to behave as though he or she were single again and refuse to take responsibility for the success of the marriage. Partners who disappear for a night or two, come home when they please, ignore the children, spend money that the family cannot afford or want to take separate holidays, exhibit a refusal to be held accountable. It is not possible to conduct a normal marriage when one of the partners refuses to be committed to the other.

Christians feel strongly that they are accountable for their behaviour, in the first instance to God, and then to each other. Yet even so, people who claim to be Christians behave in ways that bring shame, not only to their families, but to the name of Jesus Christ. For all that Christian marriages, by and large, do have a measure of accountability. But to whom are non-Christians accountable?

There was a time when a Christian consensus prevailed in society so that a measure of accountability was required from most people. This is not true to the same extent today. With the rise of individualism, the clamour for individual rights and the belief in happiness as the chief value, it is not surprising that so many marriages end in divorce.

If your partner no longer feels he or she is accountable to you, what chance is there of a genuine reconciliation?

6. Opposition to your Christian faith

We are not speaking here of the usual scorn that unbelievers direct at Christians. Many unconverted spouses are quite willing to allow their partners freedom to worship and to be Christians in the home. There may be domestic tension from time to time, but if the unsaved partner is willing to live with a Christian spouse, Scripture is clear that the marriage should continue (1 Cor. 7:12).

Opposition to the marriage partner's faith is usually an irritation to an already strained relationship. When the non-Christian partner feels threatened by the church, other Christians or the minister, he or she often makes the partner face unnecessary choices and makes demands which may impinge on the partner's Christian conscience.

Unless these matters are resolved, there can be no meaningful reconciliation. The believing partner must take a stand on these issues and, while it is not acceptable for believing partners to force their convictions unwisely or arrogantly on an unwilling spouse, they have not only the right but the duty to believe and behave as a Christian.

A word of caution may be in order here. Sometimes Christians unwisely spend all their time on church-related activities, to the detriment of family relationships. If this is a complaint brought by an unbelieving spouse, it deserves serious attention. A compromise may have to be reached in the reconciliation process. But where unbelievers obstinately set themselves against their partner's faith, there can be no reconciliation.

7. Apostasy from the faith
What happens if a professing Christian man backslides, his bad behaviour causes the break-up of his marriage and then, without any repentance or return to the Lord, he wants his believing wife to return to him? If his wife has divorced him, the divorce, however tragic, is recognised by God. The believing woman is no longer married to him. To return voluntarily and willingly to a marriage relationship with her ex-husband would be tantamount to marrying an unbeliever. This is a difficult situation that requires sensitive handling.

The same is true in a situation where divorce proceedings are in progress but not yet final. What happens if the backslidden partner wants to reinstate the marriage, without repenting of the evil that caused the separation? The answer is that there can be no final or real reconciliation.

8. An intervening marriage

Deuteronomy 24:1-4 sketches the situation of a man who divorces his wife to marry another but then finds that he still loves her and wants her back.

> If a man marries a woman who becomes displeasing to him because he finds something indecent about her, and he writes her a certificate of divorce, gives it to her and sends her from his house, and if after she leaves his house she becomes the wife of another man, and her second husband dislikes her and writes her a certificate of divorce, gives it to her and sends her from his house, or if he dies, then her first husband, who divorced her, is not allowed to marry her again after she has been defiled. That would be detestable in the eyes of the LORD. Do not bring sin upon the land the LORD your God is giving you as an inheritance.

It is particularly heart-rending to hear of a man who divorces his partner in order to pursue an affair or to have a fling. After some years and many relationships, he enters an ill-considered marriage, only to discover that he is far more disillusioned and worse off than before.

The guilty partner is filled with regret as he thinks of all he has sacrificed for the jaded and troubled life he now leads. He yearns to turn back the clock and approaches his first marriage partner again. Perhaps she still loves him and longs to take him back. After all these years, she is being vindicated. He was wrong and is now admitting it. He is prepared to divorce his present wife to marry her.

If this permissible for a Christian? The Bible seems to indicate that it is not. There is something obscene about a man who abandons his wife, has a fling, even a marriage or two, and then wants to return to his original spouse. It is frivolous and demeaning to marriage. There is a price to pay for dissolving a marriage. This was one of the reasons for constituting the bill of divorce in Old Testament times (Deut. 24). It was meant to impress on the man that this act was final. He could never have his wife back again.

Let us return to the story of Cynthia in the first chapters. After years of emotional struggle, her life was stable and fulfilling again although she was single. Her children had grown up and she had a wide circle of friends. Just as the last of the children matriculated and was preparing to leave home with all that would mean emotionally for Cynthia, Gary reappeared – a new Gary.

He was now involved with a group of Christians, attending Bible studies. His whole demeanour had changed. His life was filled with the most profound regret for all he had done. His old tenderness had returned. His apologies were profuse. More than anything, he desired to have Cynthia back. He wanted to undo, as far as possible, all the wrong he had done.

Put yourself into Cynthia's shoes for a moment. She had grown spiritually and was a highly respected member of her church community. She had developed a ministry to single people that God had blessed in a remarkable way and she had become a sought-after counsellor. Many people looked up to her as a leader. Cynthia had never stopped loving Gary. Suddenly she had the opportunity to realise her deepest hopes and dreams.

But Gary had recently remarried, after all his other relationships. As so often happens in these cases, his choice of a wife was less than he could have hoped for and far less than he had had in Cynthia. He was all for a second divorce and remarriage to Cynthia, but she knew the sanctity of marriage and the prohibition of Deuteronomy 24. Her agony knew no bounds.

We talked and prayed together. She fired question after question at me.

'What if he is born again? Doesn't that make a difference?'

'No, I'm afraid it doesn't. God values marriage too much to allow it to be dealt with so flippantly.'

Cynthia's inner tumult was so great that she became ill. At the time of writing she is sticking to her resolve to obey the Bible, and I have every reason to believe she will continue to do so.

What do we say about Cynthia's pain? And what about the children? Is God so inflexible that He will not allow this family to be reunited? Why must she suffer like this? Has she not been through enough already? From your angle and mine, the answer is yes, but how can we ever know the mind and purposes of God?

Hebrews 11 contains a list of believers who suffered anguish of many kinds because they chose faithfulness to God above the comfort of compromise with the world. I do not have answers for Cynthia. All I can do is to urge her to remain true to her convictions. I can tell her that God will neither leave nor forsake her, that somehow, I do not know how or when, she will win because she believes in God, the Father of our Lord Jesus Christ. But having said that, I can say no more. In her case the conditions of reconciliation do not meet the biblical criteria. She must wait on God.

It is important to understand that this dilemma is not the result of God's inflexibility but the consequence of man's sinful actions. Law and order must be maintained. The dignity of marriage must be preserved. Gary has no more right to break up his second marriage than he had to destroy his first. Cynthia has no more right to play a role in the dissolving of this marriage than the woman who had broken up her marriage. Even if Gary had divorced his second wife before approaching her, a reconciliation would have been unbiblical, conflicting with the revealed will of God. If they were to remarry, they would invoke Jesus' condemnation of a man who divorces his wife in order to marry another. Gary and Cynthia would be committing adultery. Cynthia's decision, though difficult, is essentially simple. She must not covet another woman's husband. As a Christian woman, she has no claim on him.

What about Cynthia's feelings, her longing and heartache? Does God not care? Yes, He does care. And we can entrust her to the compassion of an all-wise, all-knowing God, whose strong arms are underneath her. He will not fail her, nor will He desert her. If she honours Him, He will honour her. Although she pays an emotional price now, He who is just and fair will reward her in due course. But she must stand firm and not succumb to inappropriate action.

9. Unhealthy parental ties
In recent years I have become increasingly aware of

a problem that is emerging in society that causes much stress, particularly for women. I am referring to the phenomenon of men who remain under the power and influence of their mothers.

My wife was so alarmed at the increase of this problem among many of the women she was dealing with that she persuaded me to deal with it in a sermon. I was amazed at the response. For days afterwards we were approached by married and engaged couples who needed assistance in thinking through this issue.

In some South African communities there seems to be a move towards a matriarchal society. The mother-in-law rules her family with an iron rod. These strong, domineering mothers do not teach their sons the biblical principle that a man has to leave his parents' home to cleave to his wife (Gen. 2).

They vie selfishly for their son's attention and constantly make little demands to test whether he will drop everything and put them first. If the married son does not pay them enough attention, they use emotional manipulation so that he is torn between his imagined duty to his mother and the legitimate demands of his wife. Not only is this blatantly unscriptural but it is rank selfishness.

If your husband cannot put you first because he has not broken away from his own family, true reconciliation is impossible. Any woman who allows reconciliation to take place while this situation remains unchanged is guaranteeing ongoing unhappiness – for herself and for her children.

This kind of marriage partner often behaves like a teenager going through adolescent rebellion. He leaves all responsibility to his wife while he does as he pleases. Then he repents and flatters her, and she believes that he will change.

Sometimes a complicating factor is that, though a wife in this situation may complain, seek counsel and weep, she will not take action because this kind of mothering was modelled in her own home. She in turns mothers her husband who still speaks of his own mother as 'Mummy' or 'Mommy'. Family members may prevail on her to put up with it or to return to the family home.

This refusal of the man to cut ties with his parents may result in marriage breakdown. The man and his family have their own home, but emotionally he still lives with his parents. If he remains financially dependent on his mother, he will never become independent, take the lead in his marriage or become the head of his home. Emotionally he is a teenager. He flirts, behaves irresponsibly and leaves all family matters to his wife. After all, this is what his mother has done for as long as he can remember.

If unhealthy parental ties is one of the reasons why your marriage is breaking down, it is important to resist the temptation to reconcile until this difficulty has been well and truly laid to rest. It is imperative for your husband to make clear to his parents that his primary allegiance is to you.

It will be terribly difficult for him to do this. He has been emotionally manipulated for so long that he will be tormented by guilt and even fear. Confronting his family may give offence and strain the relationship with them for a while, but it must be done. He should pray that God will enable the family to see that each new family unit, while respecting their elders, must make its own way before God.

Of course this is not a problem peculiar to men. Women too sometimes find themselves unable to break from mother or father. As Jay Adams correctly points out in *Christian Living in the Home*, contrary to popular belief, the main tension point as far as in-laws are concerned is not the relationship between a son-in-law and mother-in-law, but the rivalry between a wife and her mother-in-law.

Perhaps the husband does not measure up to his strong, decisive father-in-law. He may not have achieved as much in life as his father-in-law has. This results in an ongoing feeling of inferiority and resentment. The husband feels threatened at constantly having to fight family affections to keep his wife.

Whatever the circumstances and whoever the guilty party, unless the situation is resolved, reconciliation will be a hollow experience.

10. Continued sexual relations
Many women continue to sleep with their ex-husbands, reasoning that because he is still in some way her husband and the father of her children, they are still in a sense married. This is not true, as we shall see in the discussion of our Lord's teaching on divorce. God recognises divorce. Although tragic, it is final, cancelling the marriage contract. Your ex-husband is no longer your husband. Sex with him under these circumstances is viewed by God in the same light as with a man outside marriage. It is called fornication.

A husband who can have his cake and eat it will not be

in a hurry to be reconciled. He has lost all the unwanted responsibility of caring for a wife and children, but enjoys all the privileges of marriage if he can sleep with his ex-wife when he wants to. Because many separated or divorced women still love their husbands and hope to have them back, they succumb to the pressure to have a biblically unlawful sexual relationship. The ex-husband will say all the right things to get what he wants, but he will not give up his newfound freedom easily!

Frustration builds up. Hopes and longings are kept alive, but so are anger and resentment. Constant emotional interference makes it virtually impossible to adjust to a new lifestyle. Violence may continue because the ex-husband is given access to the family. He is never confronted with the fact that he has lost his wife. Any new relationship may be spoilt or become impossible.

A post-divorce sexual relationship with the marriage partner is often accompanied by uncertainty and depression because of the instinctive feeling that something is wrong. Even if the divorce is not yet final, it is foolish to allow the privileges of marriage without the responsibilities.

Conclusion

All ten of the factors we have discussed – the refusal to communicate, absence of respect, the presence of fear, unresolved problems, a lack of commitment, opposition to your Christian faith, apostasy from the faith, an intervening marriage, unhealthy parental ties and continued sexual relations – stand in the way of true, meaningful reconciliation.

If you have been the victim of a cruel and unjustified

divorce, your spouse must recognise that they have lost you and be made to feel that loss. Their regrets, longings, memories and sentiments must be allowed to come into focus.

This can only happen if you keep yourself at arm's length. Do not give in. Do not listen to sweet talk. Any chance of a real reconciliation may be spoilt by imprudence in this important matter.

The sooner we recognise that conditions exist that make a reconciliation undesirable, if not impossible, the sooner people can get on with their lives.

'If I've tried everything to make my marriage work,' some may ask, 'and my spouse is still uncooperative, am I bound by the Scriptures to remain married? And if I do get divorced, am I forbidden every to remarry?'

These questions constitute some of the myths mentioned in the introduction to this book. To dispel them, we turn now to the divinely inspired Scriptures to see what they say.

CHAPTER 6

The teaching of the Bible

To understand accurately the teaching of the Bible on this very important topic, we need to take into account the teaching of both the Old and the New Testament. The mistake that many well-meaning people make is to base their understanding only on the words of our Lord in Matthew. They forget that Jesus always taught against the background of Old Testament understanding and the practices current in His day.

This makes the New Testament teaching on the subject of divorce an area that is surrounded by great misunderstanding and many differing views. Ward Powers, in his helpful book *Marriage and Divorce: The New Testament Teaching*, sums up the various views in three different categories.

The first group believes that *no divorce is possible*. Marriage is indissoluble and a legal divorce does not affect the status of the marriage before God. Remarriage therefore means adultery because the first marriage still stands.

The second group holds that *divorce is possible under certain circumstances*. The only acceptable grounds are usually adultery, desertion or both. Under this view, some proponents advance a number of reasons for a divorce, but differ as to whether both parties or only the innocent party may remarry.

The third group feels that lifelong monogamy is a hopeless ideal which can never be met. *Divorce should therefore be permitted without any restricting rules.* If a marriage fails, the two people concerned should learn from the experience, obtain a divorce and try again, with the hope that they will have better success.

Let us examine, as simply as possible, what I believe the Bible teaches about this very important subject. I firmly believe that much of the confusion about divorce in church circles stems from lifting Jesus' words out of the context in which they were spoken – the Jewish society in which He lived and His understanding of the Old Testament teaching. Jesus never intended His words to be distorted. To understand the New Testament teaching on divorce, and especially the teaching of Jesus, it is therefore crucial to look at one key Old Testament passage.

We quoted Deuteronomy 24:1-4 in chapter five when we talked about the impossibility of reconciliation if there has been an intervening marriage. Let us look at the passage again, this time from the perspective of the light it throws on Jesus' teaching about divorce.

Deuteronomy 24:1-4

A wife's position in ancient times was very precarious. The continuation of her marriage depended largely on the caprice of her husband. He could order her out of his home – whether she had parents to go back to or not – and take her back, virtually at will. During one of his fits of pique he could turn her out and claim he had divorced her, but on reflection he might decide that he wanted her back.

During one of these episodes, she might have married someone else. If her first husband insisted that she was still his wife, he could take her forcibly from her second husband and she would be stigmatised as an adulteress. It does not take much imagination to see the permutation of problems that could arise from the wife being the victim in the marriage relationship.

This was the practice of pagan people who lived in the wilderness around Israel. The result of their proximity was that the Israelites adopted their approach to divorce. The purpose of the legislation in the law book Deuteronomy was therefore to regularise the practices as Moses found them. Moses did not institute divorce in Israel, as if it had not taken place before. He introduced a set of controls to bring order to a chaotic and hurtful situation.

The aim of this legislation was to provide practical and moral protection for the woman. She needed physical protection from a hardhearted husband who could injure her or drag her away from a position of relative happiness and security because he considered her his own personal property. But she also needed moral protection. Her position had to be clarified. Her rejection by her husband was not necessarily because she had committed adultery. She might be a good, faithful, hard-working wife with a loutish husband who simply turned her out of the home.

Her second marriage had to be seen as a legitimate relationship, not merely a live-in one. There had to be legislation to prove that the first marriage had ended and to protect the second marriage so that her first husband could not interfere with it. She had to be given a chance at happiness.

Praise God for the compassionate way in which He cared for the socially disadvantaged in those early days! His laws always underscore the dignity of womanhood. It is we who destroy our own dignity and that of our families.

Let us look more closely at the practical and moral protection this legislation gave the woman and at what the scribes and Pharisees had done with this law by the time of Jesus.

Practical protection
A woman was protected in four practical ways by the legislation God gave Moses in Deuteronomy.

Firstly, there had to be *adequate grounds* for divorce. The husband had to find 'some uncleanness' in her. We will come back to this phrase. Suffice it to say that a man could no longer throw out his wife on a whim or a fancy. Even if the husband had adequate reason, the law did not say that he had to divorce his wife, only that he could do so.

The clause 'she finds no favour in his eyes because he has found some uncleanness in her' implies that the problem had caused considerable domestic stress and tension. He could not turn her out because he was drunk, had found someone else or they had had a minor family dispute.

Secondly, divorce now had to be *formalised in writing*. The document had to be placed into the hand of the wife by the husband himself. You can imagine that the emotion of that moment could cause a rethink of this action.

But more importantly, the woman now had a legally recognised document to say that she was free and could remarry. She could no longer be stigmatised and treated as an adulteress.

Thirdly, *these formalities took time.* The average Israelite would have to go to a scribe to have the document written. He might have to wait his turn for a day or two and this allowed a cooling-off period to rethink the matter.

Fourthly, this action *prevented the wife from returning* to her first husband after having remarried. Even if she wanted to return to him, she could not. The first marriage was dead. This legislation was therefore aimed at giving the second marriage a chance to work. It was designed to prevent a frivolous treatment of marriage, and interference by a former spouse. It kept the second marriage intact, underscoring the importance of marriage and making impossible the flippancy with which divorce had formerly taken place.

In these practical ways the woman, her reputation and her chance at future happiness were protected by God's law.

Moral protection

There are not only physical obligations in marriage. This legislation also contained moral considerations. Three issues constituted moral protection of the woman.

Firstly, *limiting the grounds* for divorce curbed its frequency. It could no longer happen on the spur of the moment and was restricted to more serious cases.

How we need to hear this today! The word 'incompatibility' is a modern invention, used to cover a multitude of frivolous reasons for divorce, the very frivolousness the Old Testament law was designed to prevent.

Secondly, written documents of divorce required the services of a scribe which added a *seriousness* and a *finality* to the process.

Thirdly, divorce *set the wife free*. If she did not remarry and decided to return to her husband, the choice was hers. But he had no automatic claim on her. If she remarried, she could never return to him. She was lost to him for ever. The husband might therefore hesitate and reconsider.

By formalising the divorce in writing and preventing the return of the wife in the event of a remarriage, adultery could be much more clearly defined. No one could accuse the woman of adultery. She was free to marry whom she chose.

Two comments concerning this very important passage of Scripture are necessary. Firstly, although this law grants divorce, it does not accord divorce any sort of status. This is a special, not a blanket permission for all divorces. The bottom line is that God hates divorce (Mal. 2:16). He hates the pain of separation but He also hates the sin that causes divorce.

However, the law provides for divorce, in the same way that motor insurance provides for car thefts, fire extinguishers for fires or first aid for injuries. This law is not saying, 'Go and get divorced'. Rather, it says, 'Divorce should not happen, but if it does, this is the way to deal with it'.

The second comment concerns the phrase about the woman being defiled after her second marriage (Deut. 24:4). This defilement was not caused by her remarriage. Some have speculated that it refers to a secret allegiance to her first husband while she was married to her second husband. It seems far more biblical, however, that this defilement refers to the fact that after the death of her second husband or her divorce from him, the woman could not return to her first husband because *to him* she was defiled.

The words 'defiled' and 'unclean' have no moral connotations, but refer to Israel's religious ceremonies and especially to whatever causes a break in fellowship between the Israelites and God.

The wife was therefore not unclean or in the wrong. The words must rather be understood in terms of her availability to her first husband. For a husband to take back his former wife who had married someone else was to engage in an action that undermined marriage and displaced God.

For him she had become unclean. He could no longer have her. She was permanently out of his reach. The *Revised English Bible* makes this point clearly:

> ' ... then her first husband who had dismissed her is not free to take her to be his wife again; for him she has become unclean.'

Marriage must not be trivialised. Partners cannot come and go at will. This legislation underscored the need for God's people to maintain a certain standard of behaviour. It formed part of the way in which Israel expressed their holiness as the people of God. In the same way, believers today are called to live by a different standard to that of the world. Certain things are inappropriate and undermine our claim to be God's people.

Divorce terminates the first marriage. It is final. Former marriage partners no longer belong to each other. While remarriage is allowed, it in turn demands total commitment to the new partner.

Interpretation of the law

We now come to the heart of the matter: what did Jesus mean when He spoke about divorce in the Gospels? To answer this question we must return to the phrase 'some uncleanness' in Deuteronomy 24:1 (NKJV).

There has been a great deal of scholarly dispute about what this phrase means because the text itself is not clear as to what constitutes something indecent in a wife. Various Bible commentators and translators have tried their hand at clarifying the phrase, with questionable success. Some have called it a 'shameful thing', others 'some unclean, unseemly thing, something repulsive'. Whatever it meant to Moses and his people has been lost in antiquity. The statement confused even the ancient Jewish theologians.

Ward Powers points out that the three main Jewish views are set out in the compilation of Jewish teachings known as the *Mishnah*. It was completed by AD 200 but reflected the teachings of earlier centuries. The relevant quotation comes from the *Mishnah Gittin* 9.10:

> The school of Shammai says: A man must not divorce his wife unless he has found unchastity in her, for it is written, *Because he hath found in her indecency in anything*. And the school of Hillel says: (He may divorce her) even if she spoiled a dish for him, for it is written, *Because he has found in her indecency* in anything. Rabbi Akiba says: Even if he found another fairer than she, for it is written, *and it shall be that she finds no favour* in his eyes ...

Shammai, Hillel and Akiba were three of the most prominent ancient rabbis. They exerted a tremendous influence in their day, especially in their views on marriage and their interpretation of the law of Moses. These wrong interpretations of the law caused a great deal of mischief and were addressed by Jesus as we see in the Gospels.

Shammai allowed no divorce except for unfaithfulness. Hillel permitted divorce for trivial offences, while Akiba went further and allowed the husband to divorce his wife for no reason whatever. If the husband fancied someone else, that constituted sufficient grounds.

Deuteronomy 24:1 did not envisage divorce without a cause. Thus Akiba, and to a lesser extent Hillel, were promoting the very evil that Deuteronomy 24 was given to avoid. The views of these three rabbis and the practices they encouraged were current in Christ's day. This was the background to the debate about divorce between Jesus and the Pharisees.

Matthew 19: 3-12

The question the Pharisees put to Jesus: 'Is it lawful for a man to divorce his wife for just any reason?' (v. 3, NKJV) was based on the teaching of Rabbis Hillel and Akiba and their exegesis of Deuteronomy 24, not on the teaching of Moses. These men had explained away the practical and moral protection God had given the wife under this law and reduced it divorce at the whim of the man. It was nothing less than permissiveness (see Mark 7:13).

In reply, Jesus quoted Genesis 1:27 and 2:24, taking his questioners back, beyond the law of Moses, to God's original plan for marriage. Marriage is part and parcel of

God's creation ordinance. God created man and woman with the desire to marry, the implicit mandate to do so and the ability to love one partner for life. Jesus' definition of godly marriage includes several crucial principles. Let us look at these.

Leave

Jesus said: 'For this reason a man shall leave his father and mother and be joined to his wife' (v. 5, NKJV). We saw in chapter 5 that problems sometimes arise with parents-in-law because this important principle has been ignored. Loyalty to your marriage partner should be the supreme allegiance of your life on earth, other than your commitment to God, and should supersede your loyalty to your children. If you build your life around your children, your are building a disastrous situation for the years ahead when your children leave home and you and your partner are left behind.

Be united

Verse 5 continues: ' ... and be joined to his wife'. The commitment between husband and wife should be like glue. This union is not only physical but social and spiritual. In other words, all aspects of living now take place with your partner as your frame of reference. This is why I believe it is abnormal for partners to take separate holidays and to want time away from each other. I believe you should resist job promotions that keep you away from home for long periods at a time.

Become one flesh

Jesus said: ' ... and the two shall become one flesh. So then, they are no longer two but one flesh' (vv. 5-6, NKJV).

The union between husband and wife is not inaugurated simply by sexual intercourse or, for that matter, through a single act of sexual intercourse before you are married. Copulation does not marry people to each other.

The biblical view is that sexual union presupposes a relationship which cements and expresses a oneness which operates on a far wider level than the physical, covering the joint lives of a man and his wife. Two whole lives are joined together.

Joined by God

Saul's daughter Michal was married to David. Saul then took her from David and gave her in marriage to another man (1 Sam. 25:44). The second marriage was patently unlawful and David insisted that she return to him (2 Sam. 2:13-16).

'Therefore what God has joined together ...' (Matt. 19:6) implies that, generally speaking, marriage must be viewed as the will of God. It is not to be taken lightly as Hillel and Akiba suggested.

I do not believe, however, that God has joined everybody together simply through the act of being married. We have to say that there are marriages that lie outside the will of God. Child, slave, trial and incestuous marriages, bigamy and polygamy are not the will of God. There are degrees of prohibition regarding marriage. For example, Leviticus 18:6-20 contains laws of sexual morality that are repeated in a slightly enlarged form in Leviticus 20:17-21.

Because sin has complicated life to such an extent, we are faced with enormously sensitive and difficult situations. We do not have all the answers and can only deal with some of these tangled relationships, with humility, calling on God for help. Sometimes things are quite obvious and we can say clearly and firmly: 'This is not of God!' At other times things are not as obvious. We must treat each marriage as a joining together by God and discourage divorce unless it is patently right in a given situation.

Separation

The separation referred to in Jesus' command: ' ... let not man separate [them]' (Matt. 19:6, NKJV) includes not only adulterous relationships involving third parties but also interference by friends and parents. 'Separate' does not refer merely to divorce but to the build-up of circumstances that cause a severing of marriage ties. Divorce gives formal status to the splitting apart of two human beings, but circumstances separate them long before the case goes to court. Many marriages are separated or split even though there is no formal divorce. Jesus forbids any man – family, friends or children – to contribute to this situation.

Can you imagine the impact of these words on the followers of Hillel and Akiba? Jesus was not contradicting Moses but rather these two rabbis whose teachings were undermining marriage in the community.

Adequate grounds

The Pharisees misquoted Moses when they said: 'Why then did Moses command to give a certificate of divorce, and to put her away?' (v. 7, NKJV). They left out the 'adequate grounds' or 'unclean thing' (Hebrew *ervath dabhar*). Moses' teaching insisted that there had to be adequate reason for divorce. The Pharisees extracted from the Deuteronomy 24 passage what suited them and presented it as though Moses had said it.

Jesus replied that Moses allowed divorce but he did not institute it (v. 8). It was already happening on a large scale. As a concession to the hardness of their hearts and cruel actions against many helpless women, Moses introduced protective legislation on God's instruction.

The law was not designed to condone divorce. It was to provide a 'fire extinguisher' to fight the fires that were already raging in the community. It was never part of God's plan for marriage to dissolve. Flippant, unnecessary, immoral divorces that taken place under the guise of God's holy legislation, but are simply an excuse for a man to get rid of his wife, are nothing less than a cover for adultery and immorality.

When Jesus said, 'Whoever divorces his wife, except for sexual immorality, and marries another, commits adultery; and whoever marries her who is divorced commits adultery' (v. 9, NKJV), He was answering the Pharisees who were quoting the erroneous teachings of Akiba, not the Old Testament Scriptures. Was He saying that all remarriage is adultery? The answer is a resounding *no!* This would contradict the Old Testament view of divorce as well as Matthew 5:17-20 and 23:1-3.

Does this mean that divorce is permitted only if adultery is committed? The answer, once again, is no. The word for 'adultery' in the original New Testament Greek is *porneia*, the root of our English word 'pornography'. It has a wider meaning than mere adultery and includes all forms of unchastity. Let me paraphrase Jesus' reply to them:

You appeal to Moses! You are right. Moses did permit divorce. He did so, not because it was part of God's plan, but because the hearts of the people were so wicked that marital anarchy reigned. Moses laid down the rule that there must be adequate grounds for divorce. The law insisted that the woman had to be protected. But you! You are divorcing your wives, not because you have any just reasons to do so, nor because of unchastity on their part, but merely because, in your perversity, you want someone else and wish to get rid of your responsibilities. This is nothing but adultery. You may try to hide it under the cloak of Moses' law, but it is sheer wickedness and adultery.

Jesus was saying that leaving one woman for another is nothing but lust and adultery. It does not cease to be that simply because it is legalised by divorce and remarriage. It is frivolous and heartless. We must recognise that the innocent party is not the adulterer – the guilty party is.

The statement mentioning adultery and unchastity is only found here and in Matthew 5:32. In these contexts Jesus is discussing the grounds mentioned in Deuteronomy 24, which had been disregarded by the scribes and Pharisees. In Mark 10:10-12 Jesus talks about the innocent wife as having adultery committed against her.

Mark 10:10-12
Let us summarise this difficult passage. Nowhere does the New Testament state that divorce is a sin. The sin consists in breaking or sundering the marriage relationship. The sins that lead up to this are condemned. Without them, there would be no divorce.

If marriage breaks down but no physical separation takes place, a sinful situation is perpetuated that results in strife and conflict. If reconciliation takes place, it is possible that the situation can be rectified. But if there is no reconciliation, the marriage cannot continue without much stress and tension. It is a distortion of biblical teaching to make divorce wrong but a broken relationship or separation right as long as it is not formalised by divorce.

Flippant divorce and remarriage based on lust and other unjustified causes make the offender guilty of adultery and harm the name and reputation of the offended party, the one who is sinned against.

Matthew 5:31-32

Matthew 5 forms part of the Sermon on the Mount in which Jesus exposed much of the hypocrisy in Israel and established the rules by which the people of God should live. Although verses 31-21 contain many similarities to the passages we have looked at, our Lord's teaching here has a slightly different emphasis.

Notice the opening words in verse 31 (NKJV):

'Furthermore it has been said ...' Although Jesus was quoting the law of Moses, He was referring to the false application of this law by Rabbis Hillel and Akiba. The practice of these men left out the 'indecency' clause. In other words, men were divorcing their wives for no good reason whatever to marry someone else.

A woman whose husband suddenly and arbitrarily divorced her and threw her out of the home usually returned to the home of her father (Lev. 22:13). Some of these women had nowhere to go and were dependent on charity. Others had the opportunity to remarry, but not all divorced women did.

Jesus was concerned to show the moral consequences of this kind of action.

> But I say to you that whoever divorces his wife for any reason except sexual immorality causes her to commit adultery, and whoever marries a woman who is divorced commits adultery (Matt. 5:32, NKJV).

The law required that there should be an act of unchastity on the part of the wife before a divorce was granted. Hillel and Akiba had skilfully done away with that requirement, yet in the minds of the people, the suspicion was always there that the woman was guilty of some misdemeanour. She was stigmatised as an adulteress. Any man who married her could be regarded as the lover who was responsible for the divorce and he too would be stigmatised as a result.

Jesus was not blaming the divorced wife but the cruel husband who had discarded her for no good reason, tarnishing her reputation and the reputation of anyone who married her. Jesus was not changing the law of Moses. He was criticising the prevailing practice which had abandoned the protection the law gave the wife, making her a social outcast.

In the Old Testament remarriage was never treated as adultery. The penalty for adultery was death (Lev. 20:10; Deut. 22:22). The Deuteronomy 24 passage was designed to show that God makes a clear distinction between adultery and a legal remarriage after divorce. Jesus was speaking against this Old Testament background and was not saying that remarriage is adultery, but rather that the unfair treatment of the wife could lead people to see her and the man who married her as adulterers.

John 4:16-19

The account of Jesus' meeting with the Samaritan woman at the well is full of instruction for us. Our Lord's words imply that marriage could, in fact, be dissolved.

This woman had had five husbands. Jesus Himself attests to that. He did not say she had had only one real husband, her first, and that her subsequent marriages were all adulterous. Divorce and remarriage could occur. Nor did Jesus say that these five men were still her husbands. Jesus speaks of the woman's marital experiences in the past tense, 'you have had five husbands' (v. 18).

This refutes the theory that people become 'one flesh' through sexual union. All five husbands were real, legally recognised husbands. She had been 'one flesh' with each of them. Jesus also draws a clear distinction between a legal marriage and a *de facto* live-in relationship – 'the one whom you now have is not your husband' (v. 18, NKJV). She was presumably having a sexual relationship with her boyfriend, but Jesus did not recognise him as her 'husband'.

Jesus' teaching

Jesus teaches that divorce is fully recognised, remarriage is permitted and a sexual relationship does not make a marriage. We also notice that a legal divorce, obtained to cover up lust so that another legal marriage can be contracted, does not do away with the accusation of adultery. Jesus insists, by implication, that the innocent party – usually the woman – must be protected. Her good name must be preserved.

Furthermore, the departing husband needs to realise before he discards his wife that this frivolous, careless, selfish act, which he might regret later, could result in his partner and the mother of his children being irrevocably lost to him.

This means that if you are divorced, that divorce is recognised by God. It may have been due to the sinful action of your spouse or they may have engineered it so that they could marry their lover, but this does not make your divorce any the less real. Remarriage shuts the door on the first relationship.

Although remarriage may be the furthest thing from your mind, your divorce frees you to remarry, provided your new relationship is a Christian one and adequate help is obtained before doing so. Jesus insists in all His teaching that the innocent one must not be treated as if he or she were guilty.

CHAPTER 7

Marriage is more than sentiment

Why did you get married?

What were the factors that influenced your decision?

What were your expectations of marriage?

What did you picture marriage to be?

Has it turned out the way you thought it would?

Can you isolate some of the reasons for your disappointment?

You may find these questions strange, but it is crucial that you answer them honestly if your hurts are to be healed. Many people get married with a very limited idea of what a lifelong commitment to a relationship entails.

Two people meet, fall in love, the relationship develops and, on the basis of a strong emotional attachment to each other, they get married. When the honeymoon is over and life settles into a routine, they may become confused and disillusioned. During the courtship and honeymoon there was a certain glow. They had something to look forward to. But what are they supposed to do now?

Life has its ups and downs. Problems have to be faced at work. The routine becomes boring. Habits and idiosyncrasies that were funny before now become problems. Tension develops and disillusionment sets in.

You panic and feel insecure, so you decide to have a baby. For a while there is great excitement, but babies grow up, with all the weariness, decisions and responsibilities that entails. Impatience and selfishness and the resulting conflict stir up panic and anxiety all over again. You decide to have a second baby, but the tension and misery persist because you did not know what marriage was when you entered the relationship.

A marriage that is based only on sentiment or strong emotional attachment usually runs into difficulties. Biblical instruction and a clear understanding of what marriage entails are necessary if a marriage is to succeed. Marriage does involve emotions, physical attraction, hopes and dreams, but it is much more than that.

Marriage is a contract

The Bible views marriage primarily as a *contract*. A covenant or contract was an agreement between two parties who made certain undertakings, laid down mutually acceptable conditions and committed themselves to the terms. The covenant theme, which runs through the Bible and has tremendous theological implications for our relationship to God, is carried over into the marriage relationship. This may sound strange to twenty-first century lovers, but we shall see how important it is.

In most countries the idea of a legal contract is maintained as far as property and assets are concerned. People manage and share their joint estate by getting married 'in community of property', 'out of community of property' or whatever the legal system happens to be. But the biblical marriage contract extends to the realm of personal care and commitment. This idea is reflected in our wedding services by the inclusion of marriage vows, even though vows have lost almost all their binding power today. In the time of Jesus a vow was a solemn, binding oath.

The Bible sees marriage as *foundational to all human society*, to be undertaken according to the laws of God. While God created man and woman to replenish the earth (Genesis 1:28), marriage was not instituted merely to propagate the human race. The essence of marriage is *companionship*. God created us in such a way that we are lonely without an intimate companion to live with and relate to.

Eve was not only Adam's helper but his companion. Proverbs 2:17 (NKJV) speaks of a woman 'who forsakes the companion of her youth, and forgets the covenant of her God.' Malachi 2:14 (NKJV) adds that 'the LORD has been witness between you and the wife of your youth, with whom you have dealt treacherously; yet she is your companion and your wife by covenant.' The companionship of marriage is protected by the fact that marriage is a contractual relationship or covenant.

An illustration of the difference between the casual way marriage is treated today and the serious view of marriage in biblical days is the process of getting engaged. For many people getting engaged panders to their sense of importance and it may merely be an act of romantic sentimentalism. An engagement can be broken at any stage, usually without serious consequences.

In ancient biblical days, an engagement was not entered into as lightly as it is today. It was the first step in a marriage contract. This contract of 'espousal' or engagement, once drawn up, could be broken only by death or divorce (Deut. 22:23-24). A broken engagement was seen as a divorce.

This is illustrated in the New Testament by the way Joseph treated his pregnant fiancée, Mary (Matt. 1:18-25). Mary a virgin, became pregnant through the miraculous intervention of the Holy Spirit. Have you ever thought about the seriousness of her condition in her day and age? Who was going to believe her incredible story of a visitation by an angel? Her fiancé Joseph certainly did not. It probably sounded, quite understandably, as if she had been unfaithful to him.

Marvin R. Vincent captures the importance of the idea behind the word 'espoused' or 'betrothed' used in Matthew 1:18 (NKJV) in *Word Studies in the New Testament*. There is an implied distinction between betrothal and marriage, but from the moment of her bretrothal, a woman was treated as married. The union could be dissolved only by divorce. Breach of faithfulness was regarded as adultery and was punishable by death (Deut. 22:23-24).

The woman's property became virtually that of her betrothed, unless he expressly renounced it. But even in that case, he was her natural heir. The marriage contract was binding from the time of engagement. For Joseph, breaking his engagement with Mary would have meant divorcing her (Matt. 1:19). This is a far cry from the practice today.

Six principles of marriage

Our view of marriage largely excludes the idea of a contract – the commitment to love and serve one another selflessly. This is the New Testament model of marriage that is described in Ephesians 5:21-33. The following principles emerge from this passage.

1. Mutual submission

Firstly, marriage involves the mutual submission of both partners as a voluntary act of companionship (vv. 21-22). Many books have stressed the hierarchal role in marriage and emphasised the headship of the man and the submission of the wife. But they overlook the comment in Ephesians 5:21: 'Submit to one another out of reverence for Christ.'

The Christian life is one of submission. In the first place it is submission to God and secondly we are in submission to each other. What does this mean? It means exactly what Paul wrote in Philippians 2:2-5a: our love for the other person controls all we do. It means that we are other-person centred. In marriage it means that your love, respect and commitment to your partner makes you want to seek their good *first*.

Can you imagine how blissful your marriage would be if this were the case? Imagine that the controlling passion in your life is to please your partner and your partner's controlling passion was to please you. Wouldn't that do away with the self-centred demands and bickering that charaterise so many homes? That is what submission to each other means.

The submission of wives (Eph. 5:22) is not meant to convey a position of subservience. It is simply a way of explaining what it means to love your husband. In other words a wife submitting to her husband, and a husband loving his wife as Christ loves the church (v. 25), are meant to convey the same idea of love illustrated by their relationship to each other. This lies at the heart of the Bible idea of companionship.

2. Order, structure and headship

Secondly, order, structure and headship emerge in the family as each partner serves the other (vv. 23-24). The idea of serving each other does not mean that there are no roles in the family. Rather, the family must be properly structured so that it can enjoy maximum happiness.

The structure and order that God gives vests the headship in the man. This was never intended to be a weapon of superiority in argument. On the contrary, the very best way we express love, harmony and happiness in our families is to adhere to the structures God gives us.

I know that the secular establishment is bringing an enormous amount of pressure to bear on conventional family living with its structured order. But many people are realising that there is no way of experiencing emotional and spiritual well-being without a return to order and structure.

When we play our rightful role, it becomes an act of love for our spouses. It provides a clearly defined framework and that in itself brings a sense of security, order and well-being. It is a relief to the wife when the husband takes loving control of family affairs. It provides a sense to freedom and draws her closer to him. It is part of what the Bible means by being a 'companion'.

3. Sacrificial love

Thirdly, sacrificial love should be extended to each other, modelled on Christ's total commitment to the church (v. 25). Christ's commitment to the church was such that

He offered Himself up as a sacrifice for her salvation. That element of sacrificial love is part of the biblical view of marriage. The exact opposite of this is seen in Abraham's shameful willingness to sacrifice his wife's honour for his own safety (Gen. 12:10-20).

Commitment to each other must extend to the point where our own interest and comfort are secondary to that of our partner. That means that it is not important to win the argument; you will never embarrass each other in company; there will never be rude and cruel put-downs. It means, quite simply, that as Christ denies Himself on our behalf, so we deny ourselves on behalf of the partner God has given us to share our lives.

4. Nurturing love

Fourthly, this nurturing, caring love includes physical and emotional nurture, care, tenderness, provision and protection (Eph. 5:28-29). This point cannot be sufficiently stressed. One of the greatest problems we encounter in marriage counselling is the feeling of women that they are not loved by their husbands. Women need to be *told* a hundred times a day that they are loved – they are made that way!

Often husbands say, 'But she knows I love her!' No, she doesn't always know it. 'But,' men say, 'I come home each night, I earn good money, I don't keep her short of cash.' That may be true, but she still needs to hear it.

Women have an inbred instinct that says, 'I want you to talk to me. Tell me I'm attractive. Touch me, speak gently to me, *show me that you care.*' This nurturing, verbal and physical love, romantic and sentimental though it may be, is a crucial factor in making your marriage work.

Men, with rare exceptions, are not talkers by nature. We tend to be silent, non-expressive, non-verbal, tough, macho creatures. We have the strange idea that all we need to do is to have a shower, apply some cologne and appear before our wives in our jockstrap and she will be ready, willing and able to comply. We are terribly shocked when she shakes her head, turns over and goes to sleep!

Have you ever wondered why you sometimes see such ugly guys with such gorgeous women? How do they do it? Let me tell you. They talk! They show that they care, with a touch of romance. You think that the most important thing is what your wife sees – hence the jockstrap! But you're wrong. It's what she hears. I am not saying that what she sees isn't important. But a woman who is not talked to, an ignored woman, an unromanced woman, is never going to be available.

Romance, words, tenderness, touching, small gifts – all these things go to make up what we call emotional nurturing. Do it, and she will be happy.

5. *Christlike love*

Fifthly, the marriage relationship should reflect Christ's relationship to the church (v. 32). Christ's love for us provides us with a model for our relationships with each other.

Christians have often forgotten that our marriages are meant to be pictures or object lessons of how Christ relates to His church. He loved her and gave Himself for her – so men ought to love their wives. The church responds in love, obedience and commitment to Christ – so wives respond to their husbands.

A stable, godly, Christlike home is a powerful evangelistic tool. This is where your children learn to understand the Fatherhood of God and the need for obedience to Him. Our homes should be a witness to our community. In these days of broken families, we should model something better. If we fail here, we fail indeed.

Throughout the Scriptures God uses the analogy of marriage to describe His relationship to His people. He is the husband; His people are His wife or bride. He accuses His people of adultery. He divorces His people, and so on. This is the language of marriage. In the New Testament we are the bride, Christ is the bridegroom. That is why in many wedding ceremonies we declare that the marriage 'signifies the mysterious union between Christ and His people.'

We need to take stock to see if this is true in our own relationship. If this element is missing, it may explain why you are facing the pain of divorce.

6. *Exclusive love*

Sixthly, marriage is a covenant or contract that ensures that both parties will be committed exclusively to each other. The companionship and commitment are to one partner and one partner only. There can be no room for a third party. A commitment in marriage means that all past relationships are over. There must be no reservations, no regrets, only a willing, voluntary and glad commitment to one partner until death parts you.

Breaking the contract

The question arises: can the marriage contract be broken? If the elements mentioned above no longer pertain, the covenant of companionship fails. An uncaring, unloving relationship damages the marriage contract because the vital ingredient of companionship has been abused. If one party reneges on the agreement and rejects all appeals to return to the conditions laid down, the contract fails.

If marriage is a legal contract between two people to love, comfort, honour and keep each other, in sickness and in health, forsaking all others, as long as they both live, when is it broken? Loving companionship is broken when abuse, adultery or abandonment enter the marriage in any of their many forms.

The anonymous woman I mentioned in the first chapter gave six reasons to get divorced. Each of these falls into one of these three categories: physical violence is abuse; child molestation is abuse; financial irresponsibility is abandonment; numerous women is adultery; drunken sex is abuse, and hatred is the result of all three. This woman's marriage contract had most definitely been broken.

No relationship can survive without respect. In a situation of ongoing abuse, respect is lost. The fact that we are created in God's image means, among other things, that we love, care for and protect the other person and stay in truthful communication with them. When truthful communication becomes verbal abuse, we are attacking the image of God in the other person and the marriage covenant is affected.

The sixth commandment says: 'You shall not murder'. The word 'murder' is used as a figure of speech to cover all forms of violence. Physical violence breaks the sixth commandment. Sin is committed and the covenant of companionship is dishonoured. It is absolutely unbiblical for any marriage to be violent or for you to stay in a home where violence is present. As a Christian, you have an obligation to seek protection for yourself and your children. It is your responsibility to retreat from such a situation. This very important issue is discussed in greater detail in chapter fourteen.

Deuteronomy 22:13-19 is an extreme example of a home in conflict. The passage implies that if a wife is victimised to this extent, the situation has to be resolved. The woman has to be protected and the offending husband punished. The woman has the right to call in her family for legal protection and public vindication, but the offending husband is not allowed to divorce her. Rather, he is reduced to virtual penury and forced to work for her for the rest of his life.

Although this passage forbids the husband to divorce her, it does not say that the wife may not divorce her husband. The contract of companionship in this case is very shaky and on trial. God places a high value on womanhood and on peace and harmony in the home. Abuse, slander and insults break the marriage contract, as does the unpredictable, uncaring behaviour of a spouse.

We saw in Deuteronomy 24:4 that if a wife was accused of indecency, the law provided for a legal divorce and remarriage. She was entitled to withdraw from the marriage and not take up the option of reconciliation because of the unpredictability of her husband.

God hates divorce (Mal. 2:16), but that is not all He hates. God hates a man who treats his wife cruelly and then, when his rage subsides and he feels remorse, wants to have sex with her. The footnote to the New International Version of this verse refers to a man covering his 'wife with violence as well as with his garment'. If this alternative is correct, as I believe it is, it refers to violence followed by sex. This is unacceptable.

A situation of ongoing violence and strife breaks the marriage contract and the woman should retreat. God has called us to live in peace (1 Cor. 7:15). If your home is the scene of continual upheaval, conflict and violence, you should retreat.

Conclusion

Several important observations arise from what we have said so far. Divorce is never commanded for any of the above offences. It is certainly permitted, but it is not commanded. In other words, if there is a genuine change in the circumstances, it may be possible for the marriage to continue.

The first step is always an attempt at reconciliation as outlined in chapter four. A Christian can only withdraw from marriage once a genuine, biblical, Christlike attempt at reconciliation has been made. If this is rebuffed, the affronted spouse who has endured abuse, adultery or abandonment must withdraw.

People sometimes present me with complex marital problems and expect step by step instructions as to what they should do. Our sin has complicated life to such an extent that it is not always easy to give cut and dried answers. We are not always sure of all the facts. Our wisdom is limited and we make errors of judgement. New facts may arise of which we are unaware.

Who is sufficient for these things? Pastors and counsellors do not have the answer for every eventuality. All we can do is to seek and apply the principles of Scripture as best as we are able. Having done this, make a decision, and pray for God's intervention and overruling.

It is possible for a marital situation to become so bad and the behaviour of one of the spouses so evil that it is more sinful to stay in the situation and allow it to continue than for the marriage to be dissolved. One need only think of the current spate of child abuse, often by fathers, or of wives who have to put up with sexual perversion because their spouses try to enact the pornographic video material they watch. The demeaning, disgusting things wives are called on to do make it impossible to continue in the home and make it imperative that they move out.

Having said all of this, I must point out another danger that may raise its head. Often a husband or wife may remain unconverted for years while the Christian partner valiantly tries to bring some semblance of Christianity into the home. They may meet with opposition or lack of cooperation. This may become an ongoing source of such frustration that they may look for a way out of the relationship.

They may envy others whose marriage relationship is loving and tender, where the whole family are united spiritually. In their envy and discontentment they may look for a way out of a marriage they consider unfulfilling, boring and unsatisfying. This is inexcusable.

This chapter must not be misread by such people or used as an excuse to do something they have always wanted to do. We must remember that marriage is more than a sentiment or emotions. It is a contract entered into before God.

Just as we have no right to abuse each other, so too we have no right to misrepresent each other and make things appear worse than they really are. We must reflect the fact that we are Christians even in the way we deal with our marriage crises. We should never underestimate the power of a Christlike lifestyle. We need to read and reread 1 Peter 3:1-7. Too often our unconverted spouses have never seen in us the inner beauty of Christ that is evident in the true and genuine believer.

With these words of caution, we move on to our next consideration: the Christian way out.

CHAPTER 8

The Christian way out

Jay Adams comments in his excellent book *Marriage, Divorce and Remarriage* that no one knows how divorce began. Its origins lie in the dusty past of human history. All we know is that when the Bible addressed it, it was already in existence. The Bible deals with a *fait accompli*. When God, through Moses, regulated divorce (Deut. 22:19; 24:1-4), it was already a well-established practice.

Adams makes an extremely important comment. He says: 'Unlike marriage, divorce is a human institution'. Did you see the importance of that? Marriage is instituted by God. It is part of His will and plan for our happiness. Divorce was not instituted but is regulated by Him. In other words, God acknowledges the existence of divorce.

This must be the stance of the Christian. We do not treat divorce lightly, nor do we simply denounce it out of hand. We must seek biblical ways of regulating it.

The fact that God regulated divorce implies His permission for certain divorces – one does not regulate that which He forbids (Adams, p. 31). God Himself permitted divorce within certain stringently defined limits. We know from our study of Deuteronomy 24:1-4 that a process is outlined. This process was meant to discourage divorce, not promote it. But it did permit it.

Remember that behind every divorce there is human sin. God not only hates divorce; He hates the sin that causes divorce. Not every divorce is sinful. Rather, the party perpetrating the events that occasion the divorce is accountable to God.

Christians should always be filled with sorrow and regret at a divorce. It is never desirable and it is never intractable – especially among Christians. Attempts should always be made to bring about meaningful reconciliation. Every effort should be made to help those contemplating divorce to consider alternative action before it is too late. However, human nature being what it is, we know that there will be times when our best efforts will fail. When there is no repentance and no willingness to obey God and deny self, divorce may be the only option.

If this is the case, how does a Christian deal with it? What happens if a Christian has tried everything with an erring partner and all has failed? What is the Christian way out? Let us assume that matters have come to a head and divorce proceedings are under way. What is a Christian called to do in this situation? How should a believer behave when faced with this kind of stress? What are the difficulties they will need to think through?

Vows

James 5:12 (NKJV) says:

> But let your 'Yes', be 'Yes', and your 'No', 'No', lest you should fall into judgement.

Matthew 5:33 (NKJV) exhorts:

> You shall not swear falsely, but shall perform your oaths to the Lord.

Because vows are serious undertakings and God holds us to them, many people find it very difficult to break their marriage vows. I recall preaching to a crowded evangelistic service about marriage and the home. I made the statement: 'Remember your marriage vows. God holds you to them'.

Unknown to me, a man who had left his wife sat in that audience. He had been going through a time of terrible anguish of conscience. He was thinking of returning to his family, but the pull of the other woman was too great. God used that random phrase to jolt him back into reality. He returned to his family and became a Christian. Years later, his family is together in Christian union. They had a second chance and made a new beginning.

But there is a higher priority than our vow to love and obey our husband or wife. We are to preserve our life and the lives and well-being of our children. We also have an obligation to preserve our dignity so that we may be respected. Respect is crucial to all relationships and must take precedence over all else. All vows to love and obey are predicated on the fact that we will be accorded safety and respect.

The respect I am referring to is not that haughtiness that has its roots in pride and superiority. Rather, it is the deep conviction that we are all created in the image of God.

In the dignified language of the old Church of England *Book of Common Prayer*, the husband promises: 'With my body I thee worship'. He places his physical prowess at his wife's disposal to love and protect her. This is a far cry from the abuse and injury caused by many husbands.

A Christian confrontation
There may be times during the divorce proceedings when confrontation becomes necessary. This must be dealt with correctly. There should be no appeasing the other for the sake of peace or for fear of dirty washing being exposed. The Christian should do what is right and not give in to sinful behaviour on the part of the spouse. On the other hand he or she should not close the door on a sincere attempt to resolve problems.

Negotiations regarding finances, assets or the children may be necessary. Enter these negotiations as a Christian, with a calm, dignified spirit of love and humility. If they drag on endlessly and confrontation becomes necessary, give calm, firm ultimatums and see them through. Whatever your spouse may do, ensure that you act as a worthy representative of our Lord and Master.

Explanations
If you are going to withdraw from the marriage, explain what is happening to the children. They are the innocent victims. It may not be possible to prevent all the hurt, fear and confusion the divorce will cause them, but a wise and prayerful explanation can go a long way in helping them cope with the break-up.

It is also important to explain what is happening to your friends and family members. Careful, honest, open communication can save a great deal of embarrassment and humiliation, and prevent speculation and hurtful remarks.

Often friends do not know how to react or what to say, especially if they are kept in the dark as to what is happening. Family members, too, are caught up in the drama. Often the parents-in-law are hurting and do not want to take sides. They may even be willing to take sides against their own offspring if he or she is in the wrong, but an explanation has to be given.

Family and friends do not have to know all the details of your personal life or the divorce, but a thoughtful explanation will help them to understand the situation and enable them to continue to relate to you.

Keep the door open

I believe that many marriages can be saved if problem-solving is approached in the right way. Often couples do not want to get divorced but are unable to reach out to each other and articulate this. They do not know how to reduce the intensity of their emotion-laden situation. Their anger, hurt or pride and the importance of saving face may be so great that the consequences of a divorce are clouded. The tragedy is compounded when the divorce need never have happened and the door was closed unnecessarily. My plea is that you keep the door to reconciliation open, even though the prospect of a real reconciliation seems remote.

I cannot promise that by keeping the door open, a last-minute reconciliation will or should happen. The conditions outlined in chapter four must be met. However, we serve a great God for whom nothing is impossible. If you are a Christian, God can save your marriage at the last minute. Even if your spouse decides not to walk through it, keep the door open. At least you will retain your Christian witness, which leads me to the next comment.

Christian conduct

For a long time before, during and after the divorce, feelings will run high. You not only have to cope with the hurt but also with the sense of outrage at the injustice of the way you have been treated. After the years of support, hardship and struggle together, you should be reaping the fruits of the hard work of earlier years. Instead you are out in the cold.

In a seminar on a biblical response to marriage breakdown, I repeatedly used the word 'dumped' to refer to the way a husband abandoned his wife. A group of women goodnaturedly took me up on the use of the word. However, on reflection, I think that this is often true. The feeling that you, as a woman, have been unceremoniously left in favour of someone else adds fuel to the fire of outrage and anger. The situation is so unfair that feelings swing from intense longing for the husband to intense hatred for the way he has treated you. During this emotionally unstable period, you may be tempted to take revenge through the courts. The tone of the letters from your partner's lawyer and the demands he makes on the family estate may goad you.

On the other hand, a husband may have worked his fingers to the bone to build a home for his family, only to find his unfaithful wife not only getting the children, her freedom and her lover, but a huge portion of what he has worked for.

If you are a Christian, you cannot give in to the temptation to retaliate. Implore God to give you much grace to conduct yourself with restraint so that there will be not spite or revenge in what you do or instruct your lawyer to do. Resist the temptation to retaliate and avoid ugliness and nastiness as Paul exhorts us to do (Rom. 12:17-21). Allow the new nature of Christ to be seen in you, even in the midst of this kind of hurt.

Bitterness and revenge leave a legacy of hatred and negative emotion that will continue to dog you. When the dust has settled, you will have to face yourself – your guilt and shame at your unchristian behaviour. You can never eradicate from your children's minds an ugly experience that was made uglier than it needed to be. Seek pastoral guidance and Christian support so that all involved – parents and in-laws, friends, colleagues, neighbours, lawyers and, above all, your spouse and his or her legal team – will see your Christian witness.

Your lawyer

I am amazed at how many Christians are loath to engage a good lawyer because of the mistaken notion that the one who sues for divorce is in the wrong.

Wives often tell me that their errant husbands have encouraged them to go to a lawyer but they are hesitant to do so because it adds to the guilt they feel about the failure of their marriage. Suing for a divorce seems to transfer the responsibility for the marriage breakdown to them when, in fact, they have done all in their power to save the marriage.

This is often the reason why the erring spouse wants the other partner to start proceedings. It seems they want to hang onto the ability to say, 'Well, it was you who divorced me!'

As a Christian you must face the unpleasant but essential task of seeking legal assistance to obtain child support and provide for yourself. You must also face the heart-rending task of dividing the assets. Even though your home is breaking up and your life is taking a new turn, you must exercise common sense. Make sure that you and your children get your fair share of the joint estate and are provided for.

Support

Tension can run high when you and your lawyer meet with your spouse and his or her lawyer to seek a financial settlement prior to the divorce. These meetings can last for hours and may be filled with acrimony. As a result, you may find yourself babbling on about your divorce to all who will give you an ear. While it is understandable, you need to realise that it becomes tiresome for those around you. Try to control this urge and choose one or two caring friends who will listen to you, support and pray with you. Uncontrolled expression of all your hurt and emotions will alienate people from you and add to your loneliness and disillusionment.

In your need for affirmation, you may quite unconsciously make your lawyer, doctor, minister or friend a substitute spouse. You may feel further hurt if they are not always there for you. You do need a wise counsellor to turn to, but make sure that you choose a mature Christian who will give you biblical guidance and not simply good suggestions.

The day of the divorce may be very traumatic. The person filing for the divorce has to appear in court before a judge to give evidence as to the cause of the marriage breakdown and the claims of both parties. Usually the spouses will have reached an agreement with regard to the settlement terms prior to the court hearing. These terms are set out in a Deed of Settlement which is handed to the court after evidence has been given. The court then grants a Decree of Divorce and makes the Deed of Settlement an Order of Court. The names of these documents may differ from place to place but they are essentially the same.

If the spouses have not reached an agreement with regard to the various claims, for example custody and maintenance, both have to appear in court to testify. The judge will decide on equitable terms. This only occurs in a small percentage of divorces, but it may have to be faced.

If you do not have to appear in court, find a trusted friend to be with you on the day your divorce is legally granted. This will give you an emotional buffer. Make similar provision for the children if they are old enough to understand what is happening. Do not underestimate the extent to which a child is affected by divorce.

The aftermath

Your self-image takes a bad knock and your confidence may be shaken by the divorce. You and the children may feel emotionally bruised. You may need funds or be faced with the shock of re-entering the job market. This may be a difficult and humiliating experience. You will need support, advice and prayer. By getting involved in a local church, you will have access to experienced pastoral help and sincere Christian friends.

Make spiritual growth a priority. From time to time you may need help as you face crises with the children. You will need help to sort out your finances and to adjust to what may be a different standard of living. But once you have settled into a routine and feel reasonably strong again, consider some way in which you can be involved in God's work. Find a place to serve.

This will help you to meet people, take the focus off yourself and fill your life with direction and meaning. It will not solve all your problems, but your life will gain new meaning. Learn to wait on the Lord to renew your strength and build you up. Ask Him to reveal the plan He has for your future.

CHAPTER 9

Remarriage

The subject of remarriage has caused so much confusion and heartache among Christians that it warrants a closer look.

It is important to say that most of the wrong and legalistic ideas about remarriage stem from the high and proper view in which marriage has traditionally been held by the church. That high view must not be abandoned. It is right and proper that marriage should be safeguarded.

Times have changed however, and sadly many of the secular values that undermine marriage have infiltrated the church. Instead of teaching the biblical ideals for marriage, many churches have drifted from God's Word. They condone various forms of sin such as lesbian and homosexual marriage, and even trial marriages or a living-together arrangement which amounts to nothing more than recognised fornication.

While I disagree with certain aspects of traditional views about remarriage, I nevertheless staunchly support the high ideals for which the church has stood through the centuries.

Remarriage after the death of a spouse

To get our bearings as we approach this important subject, let us consider remarriage in general before we discuss whether divorced persons can remarry.

The Bible appears to have no problem with remarriage as a general principle after the death of a spouse. In his discussion of the freedom Christians have from the law, Paul uses an illustration from marriage. In so doing he makes an important statement in Romans 7:3b:

> But if her husband dies, she is released from that law and is not an adulteress, even though she marries another man.

It is quite clear that remarriage under these circumstances is not wrong. Indeed, Paul goes further. In 1 Timothy 5:14 he encourages remarriage:

> So I counsel younger widows to marry, to have children, to manage their homes and to give the enemy no opportunity for slander.

This was a very practical piece of advice. All human beings are given to temptation. The early church certainly did not need scandals any more than the church does today. Widows were often looked after by the church. For them to remarry would ease the financial burden on the church. In fact remarriage was so desirable that Paul actually goes as far as *commanding* it, particularly when there was the problem of restraining sexual desire. We read in 1 Corinthians 7:8-9

> Now to the unmarried and the widows I say: It is good for them to stay unmarried, as I am. But if they cannot

control themselves, they should marry, for it is better to marry than to burn with passion.

I do not know how that command was carried out nor how it could be followed today. The point is that remarriage was looked upon very favourably in the New Testament. It is summed up succinctly by Paul in 1 Corinthians 7:39:

A woman is bound to her husband as long as he lives. But if her husband dies, she is free to marry anyone she wishes, but he must belong to the Lord.

The only qualification he gives to remarriage of widows is that her new husband 'must belong to the Lord'. He must be a Christian.

Let us turn now to the question of remarriage for those who have been divorced.

Remarriage after divorce

Many sincere Christians have either been condemned to a life of singleness or have condemned others to a life of singleness because they misunderstood the teaching of the New Testament on this subject. More particularly, they have misunderstood our Lord's words in Matthew 5 and 19 and the parallel New Testament passages. They have assumed that Jesus is warning in these passages against divorce and remarriage because remarriage automatically constitutes adultery. But this is absolutely not what Jesus was teaching.

As explained in chapter 6, Jesus was speaking about a certain practice prevalent at the time which made it easy for men to get rid of their wives for trivial reasons so that they could take another. Jesus was condemning the immorality and the low view of marriage that prevailed. To look for excuses to get rid of your partner so that you can take another does in fact constitute a legalised form of adultery.

However, we must guard against thinking that Jesus was giving the last word on the subject. That was certainly not His intention. In fact in 1 Corinthians 7:10 Paul draws a distinction between commands that were actually given by Jesus, and instructions that do not come directly from Jesus but from the Holy Spirit speaking through him as an apostle. (See 1 Cor. 7:10, 12 and 40.) In other words Paul was conscious that he was speaking by inspiration – the Holy Spirit was guiding him in teaching these early Christians how to handle the difficult situations which were occurring.

If Paul is therefore speaking by the inspiration of the Holy Spirit and giving us guidelines on marriage relationships not covered by our Lord, it is simply not true to say that the New Testament never speaks positively about the remarriage of divorced persons. Consider the words of the apostle Paul again in 1 Corinthians 7:27-28:

> Are you married? Do not seek a divorce. Are you unmarried? Do not look for a wife. But if you do marry, you have not sinned; and if a virgin marries, she has not sinned. But those who marry will face many troubles in this life, and I want to spare you this.

I have been greatly indebted to Jay Adams' book *Marriage, Divorce and Remarriage* for helping me in my thinking. He clarifies this verse for us. (Adams uses the NASB version of the Bible which translates the key word as 'released'. The NIV uses the words 'divorce' and 'unmarried'.)

There are several particulars regarding this passage that should be noted:

1. The word translated 'released' in both instances is the same word, *luo*.

2. To be *released* from a wife in the second instance must mean what it does in the first or the intended contrast that is set up would be lost.

3. It is plain that divorce is in view in both instances. Clearly, when Paul says that one must not *seek* to be released from a wife he doesn't mean by death! The release in view can mean only one thing – release by divorce. So too, the release in the second instance must refer to release from the bonds of marriage by divorce – to be 'released' is the opposite of being 'bound' to a wife.

4. Paul allows for the remarriage of those released from marriage bonds, i.e. divorced, even in a time of severe persecution when marriage, in general, is discouraged (v. 28).

5. And, to boot, he affirms that there is no sin in remarrying.

It is most important, then, to understand that the position of those who hold that under no circumstances whatever may a divorced person remarry, is totally unwarranted. This passage is fatal to that view; the Scriptures plainly contradict it when they affirm the opposite. There can be no doubt about it, the Bible allows the remarriage of some divorced persons, but not those in view in Matthew 5 and 19.

The question must be put more sharply. To call 'sin' what God expressly says is not sin (v. 28) – wittingly or unwittingly – is a serious error that cannot be ignored or lightly passed over (compare 1 Tim. 4:3). In effect, it amounts to placing the traditions of men (whose motives may be good, but whose judgement seems clouded) above the Word of the Lord by adding restrictions and burdens that God has not required us to bear. This can (and does) lead to nothing less than confusion, unrest and division in Christ's church (*Marriage, Divorce and Remarriage*, pp. 84-85).

A word of qualification needs to be given here. Not everybody who goes through a legal divorce can simply conclude they are free to remarry. If a guilty partner has sinfully engineered a divorce, there may well be an obligation on that person to work for a meaningful reconciliation. If there is any sense of right or wrong, any claim to true spirituality in the person, they must acknowledge that they ought to be married to their ex-spouse. The divorce was wrong and they ought to seek to return and to re-establish the marriage.

However, I fully realise that this is easier said than done, although I have had the pleasure and privilege of actually seeing this happen. But sin always complicates our lives and more often than not the divorce does indeed become final. Whatever the rights and wrongs may be, the marriage has ended.

In chapter thirteen I deal with the question of the

guilty partner. For now I want to address myself to the partner left behind. Although I write this largely from the woman's point of view, I am aware that all too often the hurting partner left behind to pick up the pieces is the husband. Yet for all that, as most marriage counsellors and pastors will testify, it is usually the woman who, bewildered and emotionally bruised, has to reconstruct her life.

Practical considerations

We recap by reaffirming that, even though God hates divorce, He permits it under certain circumstances because of the hardness of human hearts. In cases where divorce is permitted, remarriage is allowed too. But if a divorce has taken place on the frivolous grounds Jesus condemns, remarriage amounts to adultery.

If every attempt at a meaningful, biblical reconciliation has failed and you are divorced, you are entitled to remarry, but before you do so several important factors have to be taken into account. If your marriage failed, it would be foolish to rush into a second without resolving the issues that could have contributed to the breakdown of the first.

Let's look at some of the things you need to take into consideration before committing yourself to a new partner.

Your spiritual condition

What is your present spiritual condition? If you are still feeling spiritually low or struggling, you should not rush into a second marriage. You need time to get over the emotional devastation and to grow spiritually. You need to reflect on what went wrong in your marriage and to learn from it.

Giving yourself enough time to grow spiritually before you remarry will enable you to be more discerning about your actions and your choice of a partner. A high percentage of second marriages do not work because we tend to repeat our mistakes. As a Christian, you cannot afford another marriage failure.

Make every effort to grow in your understanding of the Scriptures and in your walk with God. A major decision like a second marriage should be made from a biblical, Christian perspective. If you are a born-again Christian, enjoying the assurance of your salvation, you will want to ensure that all your actions and decisions are made with one thing in mind: the honour and glory of God.

Your future partner
You need to be sure that your future partner is a Christian. What sort of track record do they have? Have they grown spiritually or do they simply go along with you and your church interests? As a woman, you need the added assurance that your new partner will take the lead spiritually in your relationship. You cannot carry him.

If you are taking the initiative spiritually now, what guarantee is there that this will change? Of course it is possible that your future partner will grow spiritually and develop an enthusiastic walk with God, but does he or she have the basic foundation of a spiritual understanding? Has he or she truly repented and shown real spiritual growth?

Make sure of your future partner. I am not suggesting a cold, censorious judgementalism. But be cautious so that your Christian witness will not be harmed and you will not be hurt or disappointed again.

Do not allow your loneliness or longing to overwhelm you so that your judgement is affected. Pray to God for help and discernment. If your future partner is a strong, dedicated, supportive Christian, the relationship has the potential for a meaningful marriage.

Propriety

You also need to consider the appropriateness of your actions. What might be perfectly right in and of itself may not be appropriate at a specific time. Taking a bath is a normal part of everyday life, but bathing in full public view is inappropriate. Propriety is as important in a second marriage as at other tiems, if not more so.

A number of considerations have to be borne in mind. If you remarry too soon after your divorce, you could give the impression of doing so on the rebound. Worse still, it could appear that your new relationship is not as new or as innocent as it appears to be.

The children's well-being also has to be considered. Have they come to terms with the divorce? If they really love the absent parent and are still trying to work through the emotional aftermath of the divorce, it may not be fair to present them with a new step-parent so soon.

As a man, you need to be aware of the statement you are making about your children's mother in presenting them with your new wife. Unnecessary resentment and complications could be avoided by simply paying attention to timing. Make it your goal to honour the Lord even in this matter.

Emotional freedom

In our discussion of Deuteronomy 24:4 we looked at the case of a man wanting to take back the wife he divorced for no adequate reason. The law forbade him to do so if she had remarried. We also considered the possibility of a woman remarrying without being emotionally free from her first husband. This is very real. Sometimes men and women look for their lost spouses in their new relationships. When the euphoria dies, they discover that they have married people who are completely different from their former partners. Their inner longings are not met and disillusionment sets in.

Before you undertake a second marriage, make sure that you are emotionally free from your first. It may not be possible to love your second partner exactly as you did the first, but can you love your new partner enough to spend the rest of your life with him or her? Can you honestly vow to love, honour, serve and obey, or will he or she always feel second best, constantly having to fight for your affection?

It can be most disconcerting for a new partner in a second marriage to discover that you still have a strong affection for your first spouse. Many men are called away from their new wives by their former wives to deal with problems concerning the children or matters arising out of their first marriage. This can cause a great deal of jealousy and resentment. Do you feel confident that you can cope with this situation if your new partner has to attend to problems in his or her previous family? In any second marriage there will need to be ongoing contact with the first partner, especially where children are involved. Unreasonably jealous new spouses can fill the marriage with tension if the situation is not resolved at the outset.

Apart from the possible emotional attachment to the old relationship, other emotional issues sometimes hold divorcees prisoner. You may be free from your ex-spouse but not from the members of his or her family or the circle of friends you built up together. These people all form a part of your life that lies outside the realm of your new relationship. You need to be aware of this. You may find yourself longing for some of your old contacts while your new partner feels threatened by them. Each couple has to resolve this problem for themselves. It may be necessary to reach a compromise and build a whole new circle of friends, but there has to be give and take from both sides.

Unless there is true emotional freedom from the past, it is better not to enter a new relationship that will only add to the complication of your life.

Personality problems

Many people may not have been directly responsible for the break-up of their marriage but nevertheless contributed to it. What kind of person are you? Do you have personality traits that are irritating and off-putting?

I am not suggesting that you should be perfect, but if you have personality problems or potential problems, they should be resolved before you enter a new relationship. If you are introspective and depressive, short-tempered or obsessed with cleanliness, argumentative, if you support certain causes to the extent that your family takes second place, or do not like animals or children, these things should be faced honestly.

A second marriage should be entered cautiously

and prayerfully. It is therefore as important to face any personality problems your intended spouse may have. How well do you know him or her? Will you be able to live with his or her habits, preferences and temperament? Have you talked frankly about sex and made sure that you agree about this wonderful aspect of marriage?

Do not be afraid to ask direct questions about thinking patterns, illnesses and possible substance abuse or chemical dependence. It is better to find out as much as possible about your partner before you commit yourself to a lifelong relationship with him or her than to discover problem areas after you are married.

This does not mean that you must expect your partner to be perfect. Nor should you end a promising relationship because of a problem that could easily be resolved with the necessary counselling. But do not ignore your or your new partner's personality problems simply because you have the opportunity of marrying again. Take time to talk and get to know each other, seek the counsel of others and pray about the relationship.

A healthy courtship
The events that led up to your divorce may have devastated you and your children. On the other hand, perhaps the divorce was amicable, without too much bitterness. Whatever the reason, your marriage relationship was unhealthy.

The temptation is to think that, by virtue of being an adult and having been married, you now know it all. Unfortunately none of us knows it all and we are all prone to repeat our mistakes. As a Christian adult there are certain criteria for a healthy relationship.

Respect is essential to a healthy courtship. You may have been the victim of abuse in your previous marriage. If your new partner is abusing you too, be it verbal or physical abuse, the situation will only get worse after you are married. If you are not commanding respect now, it is unlikely that you will do so later. The best solution is to end the relationship immediately. There can be no healthy courtship without respect.

Of course it is also important for you to respect your intended new spouse. If you find that you are unable to do so or you are becoming increasingly disenchanted with his or her habits, the relationship has little future. If either of you cannot respect the other, you have no basis on which to build.

Sexual purity is another ingredient of a healthy courtship. Sex outside marriage is not justified even though you are an adult. You do not need the spiritual or psychological pressure of a relationship that dishonours God and affects you spiritually. Apart from all other considerations, if you enjoy the privileges of marriage during courtship, why bother with marriage at all?

Healthy and joyous sex is personal, intimate and soul-touching and should be the final gift you offer each other in marriage. If sex was spoilt for you in your first marriage, do not make it worse by experimenting before your second marriage. Seek the help of an experienced counsellor with your partner so that you will enjoy this wonderful gift in your second marriage.

A healthy courtship requires genuine love. It is not necessary to experience the intensely romantic love of your previous marriage. Love is more than emotion. *Agape*, a Greek word used in the New Testament, describes the ultimate form of love and care that Christians have for each other. The same word is used for God's love for us that sent His Son to die on our behalf.

Christian love is an action word, not a sentiment. Our love for God and other Christians is proved by the way we seek to serve them. This kind of love is the heartbeat of marriage. Emotions should not be absent, but our emotions change as we get older. We find different ways of showing our affection. If you are contemplating a second marriage, you should feel a strong affection for your intended spouse, but you need to ask yourself whether you really love each other.

Children

It is important to talk to your children about your pending second marriage. They need to know their new step-parent and understand that he or she will not replace their other parent. Children develop amazing misconceptions if things are not explained carefully to them.

If both you and your intended spouse have children from your previous marriages, the situation will be more difficult for them. Explain to the children how they should relate to each other. The sudden invasion of their space by a new 'brother' or 'sister' can be more traumatic than we imagine. Their world may have revolved around you since your divorce. Seeing you pay attention to these strangers can produce jealousy, anger and insecurity.

The problems with children are not insolvable. Many have come to terms with equally difficult situations, and all things being equal, there is no reason why you should not. What is important is that you consider these issues before you decide to remarry. Both you and your new partner will have to work hard at accepting each other's children and building relationships with them.

Integrating two families will not be an overnight success. Bring the whole situation before the Lord in prayer. Do not be discouraged if there is confusion and resentment at first and few signs of adjustment. The family is God's idea, as is the instinctive need to belong to one. There will always be the exception, but with God's help, the adjustment can be made.

Who's who?

It is important that the roles in the home are clearly understood. As a Christian you will want to follow the biblical pattern of the man as the head of the home and the woman as his helper. These roles are not based on superiority and inferiority but on order and function.

As a woman, you may find it hard to accept the headship of your new husband over your children. You may also find it difficult to share the financial responsibility with him after being independent. As a man, you will have to take the lead with great care, gentleness and firmness in this new family God has given you. The way to lead is to serve, not to issue orders.

The matters of roles and discipline should also be resolved before you remarry. Discuss the new family rules, decide who will discipline the children and agree on the way problems will be approached. Explain the new structures carefully to the children until they understand them.

Patience and wisdom will be needed. Do not make the mistake of thinking that somehow it will all work out if you make the rules as you go along. If you do that, you will spend many miserable hours and much emotional energy putting out unnecessary fires. Rules should not be inflexible and bad rules may have to be replaced by better ones, but start with some organisation.

Privacy

Your new family will need time together without the influence of the new and old parents-in-law or the disruptive influence of your former spouses.

Schedule that time before the wedding. Determine to spend quality time together as much as circumstances allow. All the new family members and friends will have to give you room to breathe and grow. The integration of outsiders – in-laws and friends – needs to be slow and orderly so that the children are not confused and your attitude towards your new partner's ex-spouse remains right.

Finances

You may both enter the new marriage with assets, property, cash or inheritances. Beware of simply throwing everything together in a common pool. Your children may have assets and inheritances from the family of your former spouse, who may have intended certain assets for their good. Your children will grow up and ask questions. Do not prepare a fertile breeding ground for resentment and feelings of injustice.

It is a good idea to seek legal advice about these matters before your wedding to avoid acrimony with your new partner, your ex-spouse and his or her family. Talk the issue through so that everyone knows where they stand.

The same care needs to be exercised if you or your new

partner are bringing debts into the marriage. Discuss the matter honestly and openly and decide how you are going to deal with it. Debt can cause great stress, especially if one partner withholds information or facts from the other. In the glow of a new romance, these problems seem easily resolvable and relatively unimportant, but this is not so. Do not leave money matters unclarified and unresolved.

Seek help

The implication of all we have said in this chapter is that, before you remarry, you should receive premarital counselling. Neither you nor your partner should be embarrassed about seeking help. Your marriage failed the first time. Take precautions so that this will not happen again.

Do not think that because you have been through a divorce you know everything. We all need help in our marriages, from sexual matters to finances. We live in a fallen world with false expectations. As Christians our expectations must be based on the word of the living God. With His help, you can make a success of your second marriage!

I now want to discuss the problem that faces all single people – and, in a special way, divorced persons – the sex dilemma.

CHAPTER 10

The sex dilemma

God has made us sexual beings. During marriage this important part of our life is thoroughly awakened. It becomes part of the need for intimacy. A divorce does not automatically switch our sexual desires off. They are still very much alive, and for most divorcees they constitute an enormous problem. As a result many divorced people continue to sleep together or engage in other sexual encounters.

This dilemma is not limited to divorcees. Single people who have not married are also sexual creatures. Their urges and drives are just as real. In fact, sexual experimentation takes place from an early age and very young teenagers are known to practise regular sexual activity. But for divorced people the sex dilemma poses a special problem and can become an intensely emotional issue.

The Bible in no way denies our sexuality. God has created us in such a way that sexual expression can take place. What are single Christian people called to do about their sexuality? Are there biblical guidelines for their behaviour?

The first principle for a Christian is therefore not

to deny our sexuality or pretend that we do not have sexual urges and drives. But the second thing to realise is that God has designed sex for marriage and that it is practised best and enjoyed most in the framework of this relationship. Of course, sex is practised outside marriage, but the safest and most fulfilling sex is conducted according to the rules of the Creator.

The soap-opera version of sex has reduced this wonderful human activity to no more than a biological act, motivated by expediency, desire, lies and alleged love, without commitment or rules. This debases God's beautiful gift.

Dr M. O. Vincent, in his excellent book, *God, Sex and You*, underlines the secular view of sex in six sentences:

- Sex is nothing but freedom
- Sex is nothing but security
- Sex is nothing but fun
- Sex is love
- Sex is nothing
- Sex is nothing but status.

As Dr Vincent suggests, these may be oversimplifications, but they represent the prevailing mood of our time. As Christians we cannot accept the world's casual view of the sex act. Sex is much more than a biological act. It carries great significance and leaves indelible impressions.

Casual sexual relationships

Pursuing casual sexual relationships in an attempt to find companionship only results in further guilt and misery. This is not the way forward. As a Christian, casual sex will go against your spiritual interests and your conscience.

You may harden yourself to these influences for a while, but sooner or later they will catch up with you and you will be thrown into confusion and depression.

Casual sex will ruin your Christian witness. The Christian identity you have built up over the years will crumble. Bridges you have been building with your unsaved friends will come tumbling down. It may take years to regain what you lose overnight. Unconverted people watch to see whether Jesus really does stand by His people in times of crisis. You have a great responsibility in this regard.

Ultimately, casual sex is futile and unsatisfying. Your yearning for love and fulfilment will never be met by a sexual affair outside marriage. Even those who are not Christians discover this sooner or later. God has not created us to operate in this way and, although it is possible to take this route for a while, it ultimately ends in the same empty ache.

The following letter to a magazine is a sad admission of the truth that casual sex is futile. It may not represent the normal behaviour one would expect of a Christian, but for many people casual sex has become a substitute for a fulfilling, committed relationship. Although you would probably not think of engaging in the lifestyle of the writer of this letter, there are those who do. May it act as a timely warning to all those women who, in their loneliness and disillusionment, may be tempted to abandon all standards and throw caution to the wind.

Read the sobering story of a sad woman who signed her letter 'Faded and jaded':

Once upon a time I too was a flirt; young, a sexy single,

who didn't want mortgages, maternity and monotony, just the lend of a man, a good time partying and interesting weekends away.

I had a ball, thanks to all these silly, whining, defective women whose husbands needed the services of an intelligent flirt who wanted no commitments nor any snot-nosed brats to cement relationships.

I worked in a large law firm and I heard it all: boring wives who didn't understand, demanding wives who spent hard-earned cash, uninterested, non-sexual clinging wives who wouldn't let go, etc.

But as the years went by I was treated with more disrespect, even shared among my men's business associates and visiting friends, in short a callgirl who worked very hard on her back to retain her office position.

I suppose the short of it is that I was not very good at my job and knew that, so I supplemented by secretarial efforts with my body, which in the end was no big deal either because nobody ever wanted to share mortgage, maternity and monotony with me on a permanent basis.

I was used, and because I never had charged for my services I had to continue to offer them free while the wives were given expensive gifts.

I wanted a man of my own so I increasingly stuck with one who scored massively in the freebie department: free sex, free meals, free office work over weekends, free psychologist, everything free. With help from me the wife eventually found out about the relationship and left him.

To my huge surprise he tried everything to stall. I did everything to help him win over the children, and he played dirty to buy their sympathy. His wife filed for a divorce but gave him custody.

Then my duties expanded to include free house-keeping for a very demanding family pining for the woman who had thrown them away! The children's love for their mother makes them abhor me and tolerate their father.

Oh, yes, we married – he's ill and needs a free nurse who has yearly HIV tests.

The moral of the story: flirts flirt because they have nothing else to offer so they share their genitalia with Dick, Tom and Harry. Should this be a winning letter, donate the prize to an Old Age Home for Faded Flirts; the saddest race under the sun (*You*, 24 December 1992).

Self-control

In Galatians 5:22-23 Paul presents us with fruits or signs that the Holy Spirit lives in us.

But the fruit of the Spirit is love, joy, peace, longsuffering, kindness, goodness, faithfulness, gentleness, self-control. Against such there is no law (NKJV).

Self-control is probably one of the most ignored gospel imperatives of this day, but there is no short cut. The only way forward to happiness and stability is self-control.

I do not want to play down the enormous problem sexuality presents after a divorce, but unless God brings someone else into your life, there is only one thing to do and that is to exercise self-control. If you have the Holy Spirit in you, as all Christians do, you can exercise self-control. This is one of the characteristics the Holy Spirit brings into the lives of all God's children. It does no good to mope, become depressed or angry, or harbour resentment against God and life in general. You can, and must, exercise self-control.

141

The Bible has only one answer for the single Christian – self-control. There is no alternative. As a divorcee you are not called to deny your sexuality or the difficulty of being celibate for this period of your life, but to exercise self-control. God's Holy Spirit lives inside every Christian to strengthen us so that we are able to resist the temptations of the world, the flesh and the devil. Until God brings into your life a new partner who is truly committed to God and to you and who is prepared to commit him – or herself to Christian marriage, the only alternative is self-control.

Biblical safeguards

Because I realise how difficult this is for many single people, I would like to mention six reasons why a Christian person should not engage in sex outside marriage.

1. A meaningful relationship

Although the first reason may sound strange, it is not only true but immensely important. This is our instinctive need to be treated as a person in a meaningful relationship. God is a Person and has created us in His image. There is something in all of us that silently protests: I am a person, not an animal. When people use or abuse us, we not only feel devalued but we become angry. God Himself is part of an ongoing, meaningful relationship with the other members of the Trinity, the Son and the Holy Spirit.

Our unique personhood is expressed in meaningful relationships. This is what makes it so difficult to be single, because the most meaningful relationship we can enjoy, apart from our relationship with God, is with someone of the opposite sex. This relationship reaches its fulfilment in sex, the consummation of intimacy. A marriage that is filled with conflict is therefore not a meaningful relationship either.

Dr Angelo Grazioli, head of the Sex Education and Dysfunction Unit in Cape Town, points out in his lectures that the sex act comprises two distinct parts: sexual intercourse and coitus. Coitus is the biological, genital culmination or the sex act. However, contrary to popular definition, true sexual intercourse includes the interaction and communication that takes place between a man and a woman before the genital act occurs.

Gentleness, affirmation, kindness, understanding and reaching out to each other are expressions of this. In this sense, sexual intercourse not only precedes the genital act but undergirds the couple's daily life together in a relationship of love, respect and communion.

While most men are satisfied with coitus, women require the tenderness of a significant relationship – what Dr Grazioli calls sexual intercourse – relating and interreacting in love, tenderness and respect. This gives the sex act dignity and places the stamp of personhood and worth on the relationship. This is what makes us different from animals, what makes us human. Though we are fallen and imperfect, we reflect the image of God when sex takes place in this context.

Sex outside marriage satisfies a couple's physical needs for a time but leaves them emotionally empty, troubled and dissatisfied because this does not constitute a relationship. What about those who have had a longstanding relationship with someone outside marriage? While this may be better than a one-night stand, it falls short of God's ideal and will ultimately fail to satisfy.

A meaningful relationship must be based on truth. And the truth about sex is that it is meant to the culmination of a lifelong monogamous relationship. This commitment should be publicly declared by marriage and conducted on the biblical basis of respect, truth, faithfulness, tenderness and mutual serving.

Sex outside marriage, even in a longstanding relationship, is removed from the biblical basis of truth and reduced to less than God intends it to be. In all my years in the ministry I have yet to meet a woman who is completely satisfied with a live-in relationship. Some put on a brave face in defiance of biblical principles and seem content to live like this. But if there are women who feel happy, secure, satisfied, fulfilled, wanted and respected in a sexual relationship outside marriage, I have not met them.

Any casual sexual encounter that takes place outside the framework of marriage falls outside the realm of biblical truth and righteousness, reducing the significance of the relationship and making sex nothing more than a biological function . Self-control is not easy and I have great compassion for men and women who, against their will, find themselves single but still sexual. But as human beings created in the image of God, we are worth more than a meaningless relationship.

2. *Ownership*

My second comment refers to a divorced couple who continue to have sexual relations. Some men have the peculiar idea that they 'own' their family. Often when we have tried to intervene in family disputes, the retort has been: 'She is my wife and I will do with her what I like,' or, 'They are my kids and no one is going to tell me how to bring them up.'

While this ownership mentality is understandable, it is dangerous and intimidating in an unstable relationship. It is not only unbiblical but untrue. While we belong to each other in the sense of possession by commitment, this is not unconditional or without responsibility. We do not own each other. Only God owns us. No matter how much a man may say: 'She is my wife,' if she leaves and marries someone else, she is no longer his wife and he has no rights over her.

Because we belong to God, we honour our commitment to our marriage partner, to a life-long, monogamous relationship. Despite the pressures of society, couples often remain true to one partner. But a divorce severs this relationship. As a woman, if you continue to sleep with your divorced spouse, you perpetuate the ownership syndrome. Your ex-husband still feels he has a claim on you. This may result in ongoing verbal or physical abuse. You and your children will never be free to build a new life for yourselves.

3. Confusion

A third reason why you should not practise sex outside marriage, especially with your former spouse, is that it confuses three areas of your life – your status, your children and new relationships.

Your status is confused because, although you are divorced, the break is not final. Feelings of guilt are created and perpetuated so that you feel your ex-spouse is still your partner and you have no chance of adapting to your new situation.

Your children may have lived through a traumatic time only to find their world more topsy-turvy than ever. They wonder why their other parent has not left and why the arguments and fights continue. Either they resent their presence or they are given false hope of a reconciliation.

This sort of relationship also confuses any new relationship that God may bring into your life. You may meet someone who is really interested in you and expects a certain standard of behaviour from you, only for them to discover that you are still sleeping with your ex-spouse. You may even feel guilty about seeing someone new.

Sex for you as a divorcee confuses your situation and shuts the door on any meaningful new relationships.

4. Meaningful reconciliation

Fourthly, sex with a divorced partner outside marriage mitigates against a really meaningful reconciliation and the resolution of problems that caused the break-up. As mentioned in chapter five, continued sexual relations with your ex-spouse undermine their motivation to work for a reconciliation. Your absence gives your ex-spouse the opportunity to assess what life would be like without you. If you make yourself readily available, the chance of a real reconciliation may be lost.

5. Christian witness

Fifthly, you face the question of your Christian witness. All God's laws concerning purity apply to you as a single person. You are expected to live as a Christian even though you may have experienced the trauma of a divorce. The world is still watching you. While you are hurting, it is hard to remember that we are still creatures of eternity, but the Holy Spirit gives you the strength to live for God.

Ultimately, our value does not depend on whether we are married or not, but on our relationship with God. We are called to be witnesses to a lost world. Therefore our behaviour is very important. We will have no impact on a world satiated with empty sex if they see us behaving in exactly the way they do. By God's grace we must strive to set a godly example.

6. *Guilt*

Finally, let me return to the question of guilt. Your divorce may not have been your fault, yet you feel guilty about it. As we said in chapter eight, the innocent spouse often feels guilty during a divorce action and is willing to take all the blame and even make attempts at appeasement in an effort to keep the erring partner. After the divorce, the guilt is difficult to overcome, mixed, as it usually is, with a loss of confidence and self-worth.

This will be further complicated if you engage in actions that cause real guilt. False guilt can be dealt with after a time, but sex after the divorce carries real guilt that will only add to your misery. You are moral, rational and accountable. If you do something wrong, you feel guilty. This leads to depression or a hardening of your heart against God. It is very difficult to get spiritual help or maintain a meaningful walk with God under these circumstances.

Depression and hardness of heart are not the only results of guilt. Sin also brings delusion. Hardness of heart prevents you from hearing what God is saying or believing the Scriptures. You believe that your present course of action will bring your spouse back or bring a new spouse into your life, as it may do. But the basis for the relationship will be wrong and your course may be set for a new tragedy.

Sex is a very powerful human drive. God has given it to us for our enjoyment and happiness. Because of its unique dynamic, it is given within the framework of a meaningful relationship, in the commitment of marriage. To take sex out of its God-given boundaries and safeguards is to let loose one of the most powerful and destructive forces you will ever know. The irony is that sex is a gift intended for our good.

CHAPTER 11

Regret

The reasons for divorce are many and diverse. We usually associate divorce with unfaithfulness on the part of one of the spouses but this is not always the case. In the past 'incompatibility' was often cited as adequate grounds for divorce. This has been changed in recent years to the 'irretrievable breakdown' of a marriage. Incompatibility has come to mean two people who are incapable of coexistence. It is used to cover serious causes of marriage breakdown such as adultery but can also provide a convenient reason for one of the partners to escape from a marriage he or she no longer desires.

Many people live in a state of conflict and animosity without the complication of marital unfaithfulness. Because we are all sinners with flawed and fallen natures, we are all incompatible with each other. We instinctively want our own way. In marriage this is often expressed in the desire to dominate. Insults and retaliation build up such a barrier of resentment that a couple may feel that there is no way forward.

But whatever the cause of marital breakdown, the result is often a deep sense of regret. The erring partner wonders how he or she could have allowed the marriage to disintegrate with all the consequent loss and devastation for both parties. Guilt is often mixed with pity for those who have been abandoned, especially if a favourite child is involved. God has given us a conscience so that we know when our actions are wrong. Sooner or later we reach a point when we have to face our regrets.

Some years ago popular American singers Conway Twitty and Loretta Lynn teamed up to sing a song called 'We made it legal'. It displays a rare insight into the feeling that, even though we have got our way, things are not right. The poignancy of regret runs through the words.

He: Good morning, darling.
You didn't sleep well last night.
I felt your tears on my arm as they dropped.

She: I was thinking what we were doing
would always be wrong
Now it's over, but really it's not.

Both: We've made it legal but we can't make it right.

She: You're still her husband.

He: And you're still his wife.
We're together and the law says you're mine.
But we both know that God's on their side.

We thought we found a way we could win
But we both lost the day we hurt them.
When passion took over we forgot everything
But what living together would bring.

We made it legal but we can't make it right.

She: You're still her husband.

He: And you're still his wife

> We're together and the law says you're mine.
> But we both know that God's on their side.[1]

Making something legal does not necessarily make it right. Many people think that if they can end their marriage relationship legally, their conscience will be eased. Stephen Charnock, a great seventeenth-century preacher, pointed out that God has placed a rule of good and evil in man's mind. Certain natural principles operating in us force us to make choices. Whether we like it or not, we have to distinguish between good and evil. A power greater than us has placed this innate ability in our nature. God has left a witness for Himself in the heart of every man and woman.

This witness in our conscience sometimes makes us afraid. Proverbs 28:1 says: 'The wicked flee when no one pursues, but the righteous are bold as a lion.' Our conscience may rise up unexpectedly, bringing to mind actions long since forgotten. Conscience can accuse us in the midst of our forbidden pleasures. It is not afraid to denounce us when others hold us in fear, nor does it hesitate to disturb our rest when others would not dare approach us. It is part of our nature and we cannot escape it.

Often the inner devastation in the heart of a wayward partner is wrought by his or her own conscience. Let us trace a few of the regrets that surface in this way.

Causes of regret

A series of *unsatisfying relationships* can lead to regret. The grass is always greener on the other side, but when you

---

1. *We Made It Legal* by Conway Twitty and Loretta Lynn © 1978 MCA Records, Inc. Used by permission.

get there, you find that the relationship you sacrificed everything for has turned sour. This paves the way for a series of relationships, each superficial, bitter, empty and strangely unpalatable. As you become more and more disgusted with yourself, your thoughts turn to home and you wish you had never left.

There is the regret that overwhelms you as you *grow older* without your family. Life goes on, your children grow up, graduate, fall in love and get married, and all the excitement excludes you. Midlife crisis affects all of us. We want the security and comfort of a stable home. Glimpses of what we could have had fill us with regret.

Regret also results from looking back over the years and realising what *poor exchanges* you have made. An attractive spouse, a beautiful home, children you could be proud of – all abandoned for a fleeting passion and the dream of recapturing freedom, youth and romance. Instead you look back over many wasted years.

Regrets are sometimes intensified when, as a man, you come to your senses and *see your abandoned partner with new eyes*. Perhaps the years have been kind to her. Maturity has given her a subtle sensuality that you find desirable. You want her as never before, but it is too late. This beautiful woman is forever out of your reach.

Or, as a woman, regret may be underscored by a *loss of status*. Your spouse has got on in life and achieved a fair amount of success. You should be at his side to share his joy and the new dignity of achievement, but you are not. You made your choice and it has proved to be the wrong one.

Loneliness

Then, of course, there is the loneliness and longing to

have your family back. You have made a terrible mistake and desperately want to turn back the clock to recapture the lost years. This loneliness manifests itself in different ways and at different times.

Peter and I have been friends for years. He is an observant, discerning man whose sensitivity is belied by an easy-going exterior. He seldom expresses himself extravagantly. For years Peter put up with his wife's infidelities and, in spite of many attempts at meaningful reconciliation, great patience and ongoing forgiveness, the point was reached when it was plainly dishonouring to God to tolerate her behaviour.

Some years after the divorce, Peter met and married a lovely Christian woman. He retained custody of the children and a happy new family unit was formed. His ex-wife did not remarry but moved from one relationship to the next. She knew little of the most formative years of her children's lives. They preferred the stable, gentle atmosphere of Peter's new home to visits with her and her boyfriends. As the years went by and her contact with the children grew less, her life was filled with regret.

Peter was fortunate to remarry a caring, sensitive woman who handled his adolescent children, confused and hurt by the divorce, with great love and understanding. It did not take her long to win their confidence and respect. She did not present herself as their mother but urged them to love their own mother and maintain contact with her. But the warmth and caring of the new family circle made it home to them. Their own mother was no longer part of the immediate family and was inevitably excluded.

Perhaps you are experiencing this kind of rejection by your children. Peter points out five aspects of the loneliness and regret that haunt the guilty party.

1. *Exclusion* from the family may develop into *estrangement* as your children grow up. Their school, church, sport and social activities increase so that they seldom have uncommitted time to spend away from home with their biological mum or dad. They do not like being away from their friends, and forcing them to do so causes resentment.

2. If the parent who has custody of the children remarries, the children may see in the new partner an ideal role model whose views, attitudes, tastes and even sense of dress are infinitely preferable to those of their own parent. The result is that the biological parent's opinion becomes of secondary importance or even irrelevant. You may be experiencing the *hurt* of finding your role played by another.

3. Despite visiting rights and reasonable access, the biological parent is no longer part of the family unit. A subtle change takes place in the parent/child relationship. The *intimacy of parenting* is lost and a more social relationship develops.

4. This change in the relationship becomes especially clear in *times of crisis*. If, for example, your child is rushed to hospital, the parent who has custody and the new partner take him. They make the decisions and see the

child through the first traumatic hours. You are informed of what has happened as time and opportunity allow, but you are not there at the moment of crisis.

Experiences of this kind knit a family closer together but exclude and upset the ex-partner, particularly if he is the one who has to pay the bills. If this partner has no financial obligation to the children, the break may be even more complete.

5. A further regret that fills the lives of guilty parents is the *loss of their social circle*. Children make friends and as a result the parents often socialise and build lasting friendships. When a marriage breaks down, the parents who have custody of the children tend to keep the friends while the other parent finds him- or herself excluded.

But having said this, I must add that things do not necessarily follow this pattern. Sometimes the parent with custody of the children remarries and the new spouse's relationship with the children is so disastrous that they seek out the other parent. Regret is a powerful emotion and can bring so much depression and misery into our lives that is important that we make the right choices.

Forgiveness and restoration
How should a guilty partner deal with regret? Let us look at the way in which King David dealt with the aftermath of sin and shame (2 Sam. 11).

The story is well known: a desirable married man, a beautiful, vulnerable woman, an illicit affair, a pregnancy, the murder of her husband. Passion had such a hold on him, that David, the anointed king and psalmist of Israel, became guilty of the blood of an innocent man.

The prophet Nathan shocked him back into reality, confronting him with the implications of his actions. As he realised what he had done, the anguish of his heart knew no bounds. But the damage was done. Uriah was dead, Bathsheba pregnant, David's reputation tarnished – and God had been affronted.

The tragedy is that even God's people are capable of such gross sin. It should not be this way and certainly sin of this enormity is not the norm among God's people, but it can and does happen. Only those who have really known the Lord and whose consciences have been touched by the gospel can know the agony of spiritual failure.

David's inner turmoil, sorrow and regret are recorded so that we can learn from them. His anguish is made almost tangible in Psalm 51:1-5 (NKJV):

Have mercy upon me, O God,
According to Your loving kindness;
According to the multitude of Your tender mercies,
Blot out my transgressions.
Wash me thoroughly from my iniquity,
And cleanse me from my sin.

For I acknowledge my transgressions,
And my sin is ever before me.
Against You, You only, have I sinned,
And done this evil in Your sight –
That You may be found just when You speak,
And blameless when You judge.

Behold, I was brought forth in iniquity,
And in sin my mother conceived me.

Psalm 32:1-5 (NKJV) records another aspect of David's inner struggle – the knowledge of God's forgiveness:

Blessed is he whose transgression is forgiven,
Whose sin is covered.
Blessed is the man to whom the LORD does not impute iniquity,
And in whose spirit there is no deceit.

When I kept silent, my bones grew old
Through my groaning all the day long.
For day and night Your hand was heavy upon me;
My vitality was turned into the drought of summer.

I acknowledge my sin to You,
And my iniquity I have not hidden.
I said, 'I will confess my transgressions to the LORD,'
And you forgave the iniquity of my sin.

This is the message of the gospel: sin can be forgiven. God saw fit to continue to use David after he was forgiven and restored. I am not suggesting that those who sin can read into this permission to continue serving God as a high-profile Christian. But even the greatest sins that demand the deepest repentance and cause intense regret can be forgiven. You do not have to drive yourself into a spiritual dead end.

As an old man who had lived a full life that included sin and family tragedy, David could write:

The Spirit of the Lord spoke by me,
And His word was on my tongue.
The God of Israel said,

The Rock of Israel spoke to me:
'He who rules over men must be just,
Ruling in the fear of God.
And he shall be like the light
    of the morning when the sun rises,
A morning without clouds,
Like the tender grass
    springing out of the earth,
By clear shining after rain.'

'Although my house is not so with God,
Yet He has made with me
    an everlasting covenant,
Ordered in all things and secure.
For this is all my salvation
    and all my desire;
Will He not make it increase?
(2 Sam. 23:2-5, NKJV)

Another example of failure and regret is the apostle Peter. How many times have we not heard the story of the cock crowing and Peter running into the night weeping bitterly? Peter's denial of Christ was aggravated by his boasting that he was willing to go to prison and even death with Jesus. How did he deal with regret? We know that he wept bitterly, that he was confused and lonely and went back to fishing after being a disciple for three years. But then he met Jesus on the shores of the lake.

Despite his failure, Peter still loved his Master. He leapt out of the boat and swam to Jesus, a spontaneous action so characteristic of Peter. Jesus restored him by giving Peter the opportunity to confess three times that he loved Him. Three denials were forgiven by three confessions.

John gives us an interesting sidelight on the way Peter

dealt with shame and regret. When Jesus asked Peter for the third time if he loved Him, Peter replied: 'Lord, you know all things; you know that I love you' (John 21:17).

Peter appealed to Jesus' omniscience. What else could he do? He could find no words to express what he felt. He was ashamed of his boasting. All that was left was to appeal to the knowledge of the One who knew his heart. 'Lord, you know all things.' The rest of the story is well known.

Dealing with regret
Many people in the Bible sinned and were restored. Jesus forgave sinners, from Matthew the tax collector to the woman who washed His feet with her tears. What regrets are hidden in their stories, yet they found a new beginning in Christ.

Then there were those whose regrets were of such a nature that they led to disaster. Judas Iscariot dealt differently with his sin. He saw and recognised it. But he was so overwhelmed by the immensity of what he had done that he committed suicide. This is the way of despair. God's way is to acknowledge our guilt and deal with our regrets correctly.

Firstly, there should be a sincere turning to Jesus Christ for *forgiveness*. Confess your sin, take the full responsibility for it in true accountability before Him, and cast yourself on His mercy. Repentance brings forgiveness. This is the glorious message of the gospel.

Secondly, providing the conditions are right, make a cautious, prayerful, sensitive start on the process of a meaningful *reconciliation*. Time may have changed the situation considerably and made it too late for reconciliation, but a tentative approach should be adopted to see if there is a way that restoration can be made. It is worth trying.

Thirdly, if it is too late for reconciliation, take your regrets to God, repent and make whatever *restitution* is possible. Then begin, with God's help, to build a new life for yourself.

You will need help. You will have to find a church that will help you to grow spiritually and you will have to prove your sincerity. But God makes all things new. There is no reason why, guilty though you may have been, with genuine repentance and sincere faith in Christ, He should not make things new for you.

The prophet Micah said:

Who is a God like You,
Pardoning iniquity
And passing over the transgression of
    the remnant of His heritage?

He does not retain His anger for ever,
Because He delights in mercy.
He will again have compassion on us,
And will subdue our iniquities.

You will cast all our sins
Into the depths of the sea.
You will give truth to Jacob
And mercy to Abraham,
Which You have sworn to our fathers
From days of old.
(Micah 7:18-20, NKJV)

CHAPTER 12

The aftermath

Divorce leaves you single again. You may not want to remarry in a hurry, and for a while you may enjoy your singleness with its absence of stress and conflict, but most people do not choose to be single. As the healing process takes place, you may find old feelings and desires resurfacing that you thought were dead or dormant. Divorce does have an aftermath.

The single life

God's fundamental evaluation of singleness is that 'it is not good' (Gen. 2:18). The general rule is that people marry (Gen. 2:24), but this is not always the case. Paul, referring to the voluntary choice of singleness in the light of historical events and the possibility of doing more missionary work as a single person, says explicitly that the single life is good (1 Cor. 7:1).

This is not a contradiction. The Genesis passage contains a general principle concerning the human race. God has created us so that companionship and relationships are integral to our well-being. Paul underlines this, as we saw in Ephesians 5 and in his sensitive treatment of marriage and marital problems in

1 Corinthians 7. We looked at this briefly in chapter three.

In the verse quoted above, Paul is referring to those who deliberately choose singleness to serve the interest of the kingdom of God, undistracted by the responsibilities of married life. It is not incumbent on them to do so, but they may so decide. God occasionally gives the gift of celibacy to people so that they may carry out their calling. In other words, although marriage is the norm, it is possible to be single, happy and fulfilled.

Genesis 2:24 generally holds true – most people want to be married. But sin has so distorted our society that many people live lonely single lives through no choice of their own. Some never have the opportunity to marry, others suffer the death of a spouse or are divorced, while there are those who, due to physical deformity, are unable to live a normal married life (Matt. 19:12). Singleness may therefore be a painful, unwanted experience.

After a morning service in our church, an elderly lady in our congregation came into the vestry where I had gone to prayer with some of my colleagues. She was in tears. When I asked what I could do to help, she sobbed: 'Please just hug me. No one has done that for so long and I feel terrible.'

The desire to belong is immensely strong in women. This has often been illustrated in our society by films, stories and crimes of passion. A rather unusual illustration appeared in the *Weekend Argus* in February 1990. A man, with the full knowledge of his wife, placed an advertisement in the personal column:

Wanted: woman to cook, clean fish, dig worms and make love – must have a good boat and trailer.

You would think that in this day of feminism, awareness and the struggle for women's rights, and ad like that would be roundly condemned. What do you think the response was? The man's line was blocked with calls. Some women, learning that it was a joke, nevertheless asked for a date and some almost wept when they were told that they were not required.

You may smile at the silliness of a woman who would willingly become a man's servant and concubine, but it underscores the need we all have to belong. We all feel the need to communicate, to share our life with someone who loves us. We long to have someone who will compliment and admire us. We need someone to hold and touch us. The loneliness of the single life may be unbearable.

Loss of self-worth

Single people often feel left out. If you are single because you are divorced, the situation may seem worse. You may be made to feel odd by old friends who now see you as a threat to their marriage. This does not help you cope with a plummeting sense of self-worth.

The loss of self-worth is usually one of the consequences of a divorce action, especially if, as the innocent party, you have done your best to hold the marriage together. The loss of confidence and self-esteem is further complicated if you have been the victim of physical or verbal abuse. The lies, insults and accusations that have been hurled at you by your partner make you feel worthless. You feel you are not good enough for anyone to want except, possibly, as a one-night stand.

Because you were unable to keep your spouse, you assume that you must have done something wrong. You may feel ugly or old and consequently drained of self-confidence. It is natural that you will see yourself in this light.

Our self-image and consequently our self-worth is influenced by many factors. Childhood experiences, achievements and trauma affect us. Some people see themselves truly and accurately while others are arrogant and place a far greater value on themselves than they deserve. There are also those who are always unsure of themselves, appeasing people because they assume that they are wrong. Paul says:

> For I say ... to everyone who is among you, not to think of himself more highly than he ought to think, but to think soberly, as God has dealt to each one a measure of faith (Rom. 12:3, NKJV).

He does not condemn us for forming a view of ourselves. The assumption is that all of us see ourselves is a certain way. In fact, the ability to relate to others presupposes a way of seeing ourselves. The friends we make, the way we dress, the goals we pursue all reflect this.

Paul condemns a *wrong* view of ourselves. He condemns our natural tendency of pride, especially in relation to spiritual gifts and achievements, and urges us not to think too highly of ourselves. But the opposite extreme is surely just as wrong. To see ourselves as having no value does not glorify God.

There is a vast difference between being unworthy and being worthless. All of us are unworthy of God's love, grace and blessing, but nobody is worthless. Christ died for us because God considered us worth rescuing, redeeming, pardoning and sanctifying, at the cost of the life of His only Son.

Paul urges us to evaluate ourselves soberly and rightly, avoiding extremes. We must ignore other people's lies and insults. We may even need to ignore our own negative inner programming. The evaluation of our personal worth must be realistic and based on facts. Our confidence level will rise as we understand who we really are.

Paul points out that our worth is not based on looks, abilities or who is right or wrong in a dispute. Our evaluation of ourselves must be based on spiritual considerations, in accordance with the measure of faith God has given us. Although Romans 12:3 refers to the abilities God gives us with which to serve each other and honour Him, it underscores the need to see ourselves from the perspective of God's work in our lives.

Philippians 2:3 (NKJV) tells us to do nothing out of 'selfish ambition or conceit, but in lowliness of mind let each esteem others better than himself'. This is not an encouragement to behave with false humility. True Christian humility means to serve others selflessly as Jesus did (vv. 7-11).

As Christians we find our self-worth in our relationship with Jesus, not our relationship with our spouse. If we keep our eyes focused on Jesus, we may be shaken by a divorce or feel hurt and humiliated, but we need never lose our sense of worth.

To summarise, it is right to have a view of ourselves that is accurate and balanced, not puffed up with pride or so servile that we feel worthless. A right view of ourselves comes from evaluating ourselves in terms of our relationship to God, who we are in Christ, what Jesus has done for us in saving us and the glorious destiny that awaits us.

We must not believe the false accusations our spouse makes about us or judge ourselves by the failure of our marriage. Our worth is found in the value God places on us. As we believe that and appropriate it, our confidence will return and with it joy and victory over emotional defeat.

Guilt

Although you are the innocent party, you may feel that you contributed to the breakdown of your marriage. This may contain an element of truth. As stress escalated in the marriage, you may have overreacted, even though you were not the main cause of the divorce.

As a woman, you may have had a cruel, unfaithful husband tell you repeatedly that he never really loved you, that you were too young when you got married. Or he may have attacked the very core of the relationship, telling you that you were not woman enough to satisfy him, that you never really understood him or met his needs. This sort of abuse occurs only too often. One of the commonest ruses of an unfaithful partner is to condone his unfaithfulness by foisting the blame on the partner.

The emotionally devastated partner is in a state of shock. She cannot believe all this is happening to her. She seeks some explanation for her husband's behaviour. To her mind there must be a reason, so she believes all his accusations. She feels that if she can correct her shortcomings, the relationship will be restored. In this way she piles guilt upon guilt.

It is imperative to distinguish between true and false guilt. If you contributed to the breakdown of your marriage, that constitutes true guilt. It must be confessed to God so that He can forgive you. But your life will be a misery if you listen to false accusations and accept guilt that does not belong to you. You must refuse to believe false accusations and reject the pressure to feel guilty about things you have not done.

Although the problem of false guilt applies to both men and women, women are particularly prone to carrying this burden. This may be because of their greater commitment to keeping the family intact. Whatever the reason, it is important to deal with false guilt. Let us look at two principles.

Firstly, guilty partners try to rationalise their actions to cover up their own guilt. They blame the innocent party for the problems in the marriage. Counteract this by refusing to believe the accusations. Although it is emotionally draining, there is no other way.

Secondly, you have to stop seeking excuses for your unfaithful spouse's behaviour. Men and women do not always need special reasons to do the things they do other than the simple fact that they want to. As a woman, you may find it hard to accept that your spouse does not want you any more because he has found someone else. He needs no reasons for this, nor does she. Their guilty consciences will invent reasons, but they are doing what they want to do and you may have nothing whatever to do with their decision. They are the guilty ones, not you.

You will experience hurt, confusion and sorrow, but do not accept guilt that does not belong to you.

Identity and direction
As a child, you were part of a family. Identity and direction were not major concerns. Marriage opened a new world

of loving and being loved. You found new meaning, and raising your children added to this. As a woman, in spite of the ups and downs of family life and the never-ending responsibilities of raising children, you had a sense of fulfilment in caring for them, your husband and home. As a man, you found meaning in providing for and protecting your family. To be robbed of this by divorce is devastating.

Society generally assumes that people travel in pairs. It is therefore easy to conclude that life has no purpose for you as a single person. As a woman, you have been identified with your husband, his life, job, friends, hopes and dreams. His fortunes and misfortunes were yours. It is therefore not surprising that you feel as if you do not really know who you are or what you should be doing with your life after the divorce.

Resist the urge to panic as you face this overwhelming sense of disaster, fear and meaninglessness. Find a friend who will act as an anchor and be assured that this traumatic period will pass. Your life will come together again.

The temptation in this period is to search anxiously for a relationship or things to do. 'Panic' decisions have 'panic' results. As you realise that things will improve, you will not be stampeded into seeking significance in the wrong places or with the wrong people.

Take time to find yourself and a new sense of direction. Your identity does not lie only in the strange, wonderful uniqueness that makes you who you are, but in your relationship with God. Jesus is not only your Saviour and Redeemer but also your Shepherd, Brother and Friend. As you hold onto Him with the determination to keep spiritually strong and growing, you will need to find new goals. You may be surprised to see what doors will open for you. Do not lose heart.

Moods

The period of adjustment after your divorce and the struggle to find a new identity may be accompanied by severe mood swings. It may take time to regain control of your emotions.

You may feel hostile towards God for allowing this situation to develop. After all, could He not have stopped it? This anger with God will add to your guilt because you know you should not feel this way. At times your anger may be directed at your ex-spouse, their new partner or even your children, to be followed by deep remorse and the ever-present guilt.

Sometimes you will be depressed by the nagging fear that you will be alone for ever, rejected and unwanted. Your mirror shows that you are ageing and you wonder, as a woman, if anyone will find you attractive again. You experience a great surge of hope when you meet someone you like and relief that he finds you attractive. His attention will flatter and encourage you. If his attentions wane, you may find your emotions swinging wildly again.

This period of emotional adjustment can be so severe that you may feel God is punishing you for long-forgotten sins. The pendulum of your emotions may swing out of control as you battle to come to terms with the single life, but do not panic! Equilibrium will come. Rest in the knowledge that your life is in God's hands.

Child-raising

A single parent is faced with the struggles of raising a child alone. Child-raising is no easy task at the best of times; without the regular support of a partner, you may feel that you will not manage. You may have the added burden of a malicious partner undoing in one weekend all you have been trying to achieve with the child during the week.

While this is not a comprehensive treatment of the subject, you may find the following *do's* and *don'ts* helpful.

Don'ts

Don't use your children as instruments of revenge. Unfortunately parents often do this. The children have been traumatised by the pre-divorce conflict, the divorce itself and the immediate emotional aftermath. They do not need to be used as a weapon to get at the other parent.

Don't use your children to spy when they go to your former spouse's home.

Don't encourage them to take sides against your ex-spouse. They are confused enough already.

Don't use your children as shoulders to cry on. There will be times when emotional burdens need to be shared, but they are only children, also trying to cope. Share your burdens with an adult friend.

Don't fall into the trap of making your children the focus of your life even though it is perfectly understandable that you will want to pull your little family together after this great hurt. They need to grow up normally. If your own insecurity drives you to develop unhealthy relationships with them, you will stifle them. Your children will eventually grow up and leave home and you will be on your own again. You must therefore seek your own circle of friends.

Don't become disorganised. If your children are young, try to keep them in a routine. If everything seems to be out of control, this only leads to greater depression and insecurity. Your children desperately need to know that somebody is still in control. That person must be you.

You may face the unpleasantness of your ex-spouse lying about you, undermining or scorning you to your children when they spend time together. Your children may come back rude, cheeky, unruly, angry and embittered. Deal with this firmly and continue to pray for them. Work at undoing the harm your ex-spouse has done. You may feel that you will never win the battle, but remember that your children love both of you. They do not know who to believe. They may know that the things they have heard are lies and may be angry about them, not with you.

Don't lose your dignity. Quietly, firmly, lovingly and prayerfully, in dependence on God, keep teaching them what is right.

Don't lie to your children about finances and relationships. Be honest! They need to know why they cannot have what other children have. They also need straight answers about the new friend you are spending time with. Deal openly and honestly with questions, fears and resentments.

Don't panic at the changes that accompany growing up or be caught off guard by these emotional swings. Remember that your children are growing up and changing. Their moods may swing and their allegiance to you may change. They may suddenly announce that they want to live with your ex-spouse. This may devastate you because you feel you are losing them too.

Don't be angry or upset. At times a child needs his father and at other times his mother.

Don't allow unnecessary changes, but at the same time, do not resist those that are necessary. If the children need to move to your spouse's house, you will need wisdom and strength to deal with this.

Positive action

Keep some positive action in mind for dealing with your children as a single parent. As the father of three children, I find that the older I get, the less I seem to know. I have made my fair share of mistakes, but allow me to make seven suggestions to those who are struggling with raising children alone.

1. *Read* all you can lay your hands on. Much excellent material is available from the experts. Your local Christian bookstore is a good place to start.

2. Persist in *teaching your children what is right*. Give Christian instruction and, as long as they are under your control, insist that they go to church or Sunday School.

    Resist the foolish notion that they must make up their own minds about their spiritual welfare. You do not let them decide whether to see a doctor when they are ill or whether to go to school. How much more do they need firm control about their spiritual welfare? When they grow up, you can no longer influence them and the opportunity to win them for Christ is lost. Keep teaching them about Jesus and His love.

3. Keep on *praying* for your children. Take

each to God by name. Remind God of your circumstances. Ask Him to have mercy on your children, to overrule the disaster of the divorce and to give them the gift of eternal life. Never give up on them.

4. Remember *discipline*. Do not give in to pity because they have been through so much. Explain their routine and keep to it. Make sure that they know what the penalties are for disobedience. Even though it may be difficult, maintain discipline. If you are honestly perplexed about the validity of discipline or the extent of it, do not hesitate to seek out your pastor, a trusted friend or counsellor for help and guidance.

5. Your children need to *develop their own personalities*. Allow them enough space to be themselves and be sensitive to their need for privacy. You cannot watch over or protect them for ever or live their lives for them. The time will come when you are no longer responsible for their decisions.

6. Do not be embarrassed to *seek help* with your children from time to time. If possible, make your ex-spouse take their share of the responsibility. Talk to their teachers. But above all, seek biblical and spiritual counsel from people you have identified as wise and experienced Christians.

7. *Keep your cool.* Raising children, with all their emotions, school problems, sicknesses and

social activities, is exhausting. It is doubly so if you have to manage alone. You will suffer from fatigue from time to time and feel that you are at the end of your tether. Believe that you and your children will survive. I used to pray: 'Lord, help me to survive my kids and my kids to survive me.' To date He has granted my request!

Right responses

Sexual pressures at work, the irritation of coping with well-meaning matchmakers, uncertainty about how to behave with the opposite sex and, in some circles, the social prejudice against singles raise an important question: how do I respond as a single person? You may be single through no choice of your own and may feel unsure as to how to respond in certain circumstances. Let me make a few suggestions.

Self-worth

Casual sexual relationships are not an option. You are worth more than that. Place a high value on yourself as God's child, created in His image. It may not be your fault that you are single. No one can manufacture a partner for you. Trust God to undertake for you. Do not panic or get angry, resentful or impatient. Concentrate on growing in your relationship to God and entrust your desires to Him.

A healthy self-image, for a Christian, does not mean an emphasis on self-importance or personal rights. The only identity that has eternal worth lies in being a child of God. To be a Christian means that our sins have been forgiven and we are bona fide members of God's family. We have an eternal inheritance and the Holy Spirit assures us that we belong to God. He has taken up residence in our bodies which are the temple of God. A glorious destiny awaits us as we discover our true identity in Him. You do not have to boost your self-image by having a relationship with someone, especially if it is a relationship that dishonours God.

Seek God's kingdom

Christians do not seek self-worth as an end in itself. Such a search is hopeless. Our starting point, in the words of the Master, is to 'seek first the kingdom of God and His righteousness, and all these things shall be added to you' (Matt. 6:33, NKJV). All the things we need that make us feel significant and happy are a by-product of seeking first the glory of God and His will and showing, by the way we live, that we are members of His kingdom. Jesus said: 'He who finds his life will lose it, and he who loses his life for my sake will find it' (Matt. 10:39, NKJV).

This is an immensely important principle for happiness and fulfilment. As we abandon our selfishness and lose ourselves in seeking to serve others, we reflect the nature of the Lord Jesus Himself. He has given a special promise to those who seek to honour Him in this way:

> He who has My commandments and keeps them, it is he who loves Me. And he who loves Me will be loved by My Father, and I will love him and manifest Myself to him (John 14:21, NKJV).

Have you not wished that Jesus would make Himself known to you in a special way, that He would talk to you and assure you of His love and presence? He promises that He will 'show Himself' to those who love Him and keep His commandments.

Prayer

Right responses are forged in us as we wait prayerfully on God. What else can we do? Though we may fume and rage, weep, despair and become depressed, this will not change our situation. We need to entrust ourselves to our Father in heaven and, as King David of Israel learnt, wait on God in the midst of our struggles (Ps. 27:14).

Prayer is so important, yet we find it such a difficult spiritual exercise. Perhaps the heart of the struggle is unbelief. We seldom recognise this and many sincere Christians would be affronted if we suggested that the reason for their apathy about prayer is unbelief. Let me clarify this. When we approach God in prayer, we are immediately confronted by two questions: Does God hear me? Will He answer my prayer?

To a non-Christian or irreligious person, prayer must seem a ridiculous activity. We appear to be talking to nothing, pleading for something we want. Judging by past experience, we ourselves may feel that all our prayers are to no avail.

King David seems to have had a similar experience. He learnt that waiting is part of the prayer experience. God's dealing with us in prayer can sometimes only be judged over a period of time and not prayer by prayer or request by request.

Cultivate the right responses to the pressures you experience. Do the thing that honours God. Be strong and take heart – know that God will not fail you.

Healing steps

Let us look at a few practical steps on the road to healing and acceptance of your new circumstances.

Support groups

Belonging to a support group can be invaluable in helping you to come to terms with and adjust to the single life, but you need to be aware of two dangers in secular groups of this nature. The first is people on the prowl for someone sad and vulnerable. The second is that secular groups do not have the spiritual resources of Christian groups. They often degenerate into a pooling of bitterness, with people not relating to each other very well nor coming to terms with their situations positively and creatively.

As a Christian you cannot afford to squander your emotional reserves in this way. If your church has no support group for people who are facing your particular difficulties, consider starting one yourself. You probably know others facing the same hurt and problems who are also looking for help. As you think about starting such a fellowship, bear three things in mind.

Your fellowship must be centred around the Bible. You need to know what God is saying to you. You have probably had enough of the advice of friends and family. Searching the Scriptures together will provide genuine comfort and guidance. Select some of the many books and study guides available to help you (see Bibliography), but do not focus only on divorce, singleness and its related problems. Wholesome exposition of the Bible with the help of a good commentary will meet your deeper needs and strengthen your relationship with the Father.

Be sure that your fellowship does not become a lonely

hearts club! The Christian church has its fair share of social misfits, many of whom will be drawn to a fellowship of this nature. The knowledge that the group is concerned about spiritual matters and centred on the Bible acts as a screen that deters people with ulterior motives from coming.

As you open your home and your heart, you will find yourself ministering to the needs of others. While it is good to draw on your own experience, you will find the need to know more than that. Seek training in counselling others. Shop around for training courses, read books, make enquiries.

God may use your divorce to launch you into a ministry that will change your life and bless countless others.

Homemaking
The need to create a new home for yourself and your children offers a wonderful opportunity to make a fresh start. Do not let your hurt spill over into untidy surroundings. This will only intensify your feeling of being out of control. Begin to express your personality in the way you furnish your flat or house.

As a single man you may have to learn to do things you have never done before – washing, cooking, cleaning. See it as a challenge. Let your home be a witness to others. You will feel better if you live in attractive surroundings.

Dress
The same applies to the way you dress. I have seen men and women let themselves go in marriage. They no longer feel the need to look attractive and become undisciplined and untidy. During the separation prior to divorce, they

lose weight, dress well and generally smarten up, only to let themselves go again after a reconciliation. Others allow their depression to get on top of them so that they pay no attention to personal appearance.

Part of building self-respect is taking care of yourself. If you look good, dress attractively and take care of yourself, you will feel better about yourself. This does not mean that you have to go overboard or spend more than you can afford. But the better you look, the better you will feel about yourself. Dignity and self-respect will make it easier for you to accept yourself and for others to accept and respect you.

CHAPTER *13*

Questions and answers

Some questions may arise during the period of separation or while preparations are being made to institute a divorce action. Others arise during the divorce proceedings or after the divorce has been finalised. They may be the result of the offended spouse feeling guilty about the divorce or because the two people still love each other even though a great deal of unhappiness has passed between them. On the other hand, the guilty partner may suddenly realise, too late, what he or she has allowed to happen.

What must I do if my partner gets converted?

Sometimes this question is asked in the fear that the person will have to go back to an unbearable situation. Sometimes it is asked with the real hope that the family may be reunited. How wonderful it would be to see divorce avoided because the erring spouse has found Christ!

If the guilty party is truly converted, we rejoice and thank God for His kindness in answering prayer. But this does not mean that the divorce action is immediately scrapped. Many guilty spouses feign a spiritual conversion to get their partner back. The claim must therefore be treated with discernment. To be so relieved at the prospect of reconciliation that you throw all caution to the wind may have unhappy consequences. After a week or two back together you may discover that the conversion was faked and all the old problems have resurfaced.

Do not stop any proceedings on the grounds of a professed conversion experience. Insist that your partner prove his or her spiritual bona fides. Look for evidence, speak to friends who know both of you, be critical, but hopeful. Divorce proceedings can be suspended for a while without cancelling them. Keep your options open until you are convinced that the conversion is real.

If the conversion is genuine, there is not only hope for a meaningful reconciliation but the obligation to seek it with the help of an experienced marriage counsellor. It is of the utmost importance to address the issues that led to the breakdown of the marriage. All the problems that existed previously must be dealt with biblically and prayerfully.

Why do I feel so guilty?

I have yet to meet a person who, pending a divorce, did not feel guilty. Most women feel guilty about the breakdown of their marriages even though they are innocent. Some have been verbally abuse for so long that they believe the things their husbands say about them. Their self-esteem is so low that they have few or no emotional or psychological resources to see them through the trauma of a divorce and they sink into depression and guilt.

Counsellors must guard against being so sympathetic to the injured spouse that they overlook their contribution to the marriage breakdown. As a marriage deteriorates, retaliation, hurt and sometimes spite make both parties guilty. If you have consistently worked, fought, prayed and pleaded for the marriage in every conceivable way, and let your spouse know that you do not want a divorce, there comes a time when you can no longer accept the blame for the failure of the marriage.

You may be hurt, you may have regrets about some of the things you have said and done, but if your partner no longer wants you, your home or your children, there is nothing more you can do. Accept legitimate guilt, but reject false guilt. Wallowing in it will only hinder your recovery.

Why do I feel so sorry for him?

Women usually ask this question. Husbands who never believed that their wives would leave are sometimes so shocked when they do that they react emotionally. They weep and plead with their wives to take them back. Some women are very susceptible to this. They pity their husbands, feel guilty and want to mother them. If the husband gets ill during this period, it increases the emotional pressure on the wife.

An errant spouse does not need pity, mothering or sympathy. He needs repentance. If you give in at this crucial time, you may end up with a meaningless reconciliation without any of the problems being solved. Pray for your partner, but do not go back until he has agreed to work towards a meaningful reconciliation (see ch. 4).

What will happen to my guilty partner?

I have dealt with this question in some detail at the end of this chapter. Suffice it to say that the party responsible for the break-up of the marriage carries their guilt until they come to the Lord Jesus for forgiveness. When they do so, as with all sin, they will be forgiven and cleansed from all guilt.

That does not mean that their sin will have no consequences. Hurt and scars may remain, but in Christ there is hope even for the guilty party.

Why do I feel as though my ex-spouse still owns me?

Divorced people sometimes feel as though they still own each other even though they have been divorced for some time. This is made worse when children are involved. The marriage partners speak to each other as if they are still married and sometimes still sleep together.

If you are a Christian, this cannot be part of your lifestyle. Divorced people no longer belong to each other. There may be legal obligations to be fulfilled with regard to the children, but there can be no ownership of each other. To allow free entry into your home, verbal or physical abuse or a sexual relationship is to negate the very thing the divorce was meant to provide – safety, peace and dignity. This is contrary to the biblical principles of divorce.

Insist that the terms of the divorce are kept as far as visiting rights for the children are concerned. Do not allow your ex-spouse into your home whenever they please. Insist on respect and walk away from abuse. If necessary, lay a charge against physical abuse. Until the fact that you no longer belong to each other is established, the situation cannot be resolved.

Why did God allow this to happen?

I wish I could answer this question adequately, but

I cannot. All we can say is that God hates divorce. He is not the author of sin and cannot be blamed for it.

We know that all things work together for the good to those who love Him and are called according to his purpose (Rom. 8:28). This means that God orders everything so that it will turn out for your good. What an amazing thought! The God of history controls everything that happens in His universe so that it will work for the good of those He has called, including you!

God has a plan for each of our lives. If you are a Christian, God loved you even before you were born. He chose you according to His purpose – to save from this world a people who are called by His name. You are a part of His worldwide family. You may sometimes feel that you do not love Him or that your love is very weak. Despite these emotional reactions, He has called you, and you are His for ever.

You may wonder how your unhappy marriage, your divorce and sadness, your confused, hurt children can all be used by God for your good. God has the power to do things you never dreamed possible. His primary concern is your spiritual welfare. Somehow, in the welter of hurt and confusion, although you may not know it, you are growing. Trust Him and ask Him to give you the strength to hold on.

Why should I forgive my ex-spouse?
While many people are able to settle their divorces amicably and live relatively tension-free lives, others are hurt so deeply and their feelings run so high that each meeting with the divorced spouse is filled with tension. How should you treat the person who devastated your life? God calls you to learn to forgive them.

Dr Jay Adams points out in *The Christian Counsellor's Manual* that the Scriptures do not command us to forgive and forget, because we do not have the ability to 'forget' at will. Forgiveness is not like shock treatment that wipes out unpleasant memories of the past. For the Christian, forgiveness is a decision, not a feeling. We choose to grant forgiveness as God commands because He has forgiven us (Matt. 6:14-15).

This does not mean that we forget all the hurt of the past. It simply means that, because we are Christians, we do not dwell on it or raise it with the guilty party at every opportunity we get. This forgiveness is unconditional, just as Christ's forgiveness of us is unconditional. It is a decision we make without looking for or expecting a response from our partner.

You must act with dignity, displaying the spirit of the Lord Jesus Christ towards your ex-spouse, even if he or she continues to live as before.

Gary Collins points out in *Christian Counselling* how hard it is to shed the idea that we must pay for our sins. We may feel, quite unconsciously, that our guilty spouse has not paid for their sins. Instead of leaving them to God, we try to take over the job of making them pay. Our unfriendliness, aggressive attitude and sarcasm are constant reminders of how repulsive they are to us. The better way is to take our hurts and memories to God and to leave them there. Our guilty spouse is accountable to God, who knows how to deal with them.

Let us keep our Christian dignity and equilibrium and deal with them as we would any other human being – with respect. The in-dwelling Holy Spirit whom the Lord Jesus Christ has sent to be our Comforter and Friend gives us the strength to glorify God even in the hard things of life.

What if my partner isn't a Christian?
Many Christians live with spouses who do not understand or appreciate their Christian faith, but nevertheless love and accept them. The fact that your spouse is unsaved does not constitute grounds for divorce. Let us look at practical ways in which a Christian can improve and protect his or her marriage with an unsaved partner.

It is both arrogant and erroneous to assume that only Christians can be good marriage partners and parents. Many men and women who are not born-again believers make very devoted life partners and parents. In fact, Christians are often shown up rather badly by their unsaved spouses.

It is true that a sincere, growing Christian should add a new dimension to the role of spouse and parent, but we must not assume that our unconverted partners cannot fulfil these roles successfully. It is important to give credit where credit is due.

A Christian spouse should be fully committed to his or her unsaved partner. The fact that your partner is unsaved does not mean that you have to be unhappy. You can work at and expect your marriage to be happy and fulfilling. Your unconverted partner should feel loved and respected and be encouraged to reach their full potential.

Do not fall into the trap of expecting less of them because they do not believe. They may not be able to understand or appreciate all you do or believe. In fact, they may object to some of your activities, but offer encouragement all the way.

Converting your spouse is God's work, not yours. Your responsibility is to be faithful and caring, always remembering to pray for them. As you are natural, genuine, sincere and loyal, enjoying your marriage, their resistance to Christianity will be softened. Doing foolish things that make them feel like the object of a domestic evangelistic campaign will alienate rather than win them for Christ.

Many husbands feel a sense of rivalry with the church. This is especially true if, as a woman, you became a Christian after some years of marriage. At first, he may be glad that you have found something to do and he may approve of your church involvement. He may even be secretly proud of you. But when he discovers how serious you are, his feelings may turn to jealousy. Try to allay his fears.

Clashes will arise from time to time, but problems are part of life and are meant to be solved. Problems are growth opportunities, not excuses to walk out or get divorced. There may, however, be times when your unconverted partner makes demands on you that are clearly contrary to your Christian conscience. When this happens, you must humbly and carefully put God first. Commit the matter to Him in prayer and trust Him to work it out.

Don'ts
Permit me to list a few *don'ts* that pertain to this situation.

Don't make your marriage partner's salvation your responsibility. You should be concerned for their salvation and you should witness sensitively and compassionately when the opportunity arises, by word and with your life

(1 Pet. 3:1-2). But in the final analysis, the work in their heart must be done by the Holy Spirit.

Don't give in to spiritual loneliness and self-pity. If you are the only Christian in the family and your partner does not help you care for the spiritual well-being of the family, you may feel stranded in your attempts to bring real Christian standards into your home. Instead of encouraging the children to go to Sunday School, your partner may suggest some other activity. This is what being a Christian is all about. Don't feel sorry for yourself!

Don't idealise marriage. No marriage is perfect. If you have the idea that all your problems will disappear if your partner becomes a Christian, you will only be disillusioned. It is foolish to endanger a perfectly good marriage by fantasising about an impossible ideal that can never be realised.

Don't adopt a demeanour that puts your unsaved partner off. Attacking them for their lack of spiritual interest or nagging them to go to church does more harm than good. There will be times when you may have to remind them of their responsibilities, but this should be done in a meek, Christlike manner. Prayer is much more effective than unattractive behaviour.

As a woman, *don't* blame your partner for withdrawing. If he takes a backseat because you tend to be a more upfront person, it is easy to become pushy without realising it. You take decisions out of his hands until you are the one who takes the initiative in everything. Pushiness will cause your spouse to withdraw even further. Help him to feel that he is the head of the home.

Don't flaunt your spirituality. Letting your unsaved partner know how much God is using you, and how devout you are, has all sorts of negative results. They may dig in their heels and become unreasonable even though they are usually reasonable. They may refuse to communicate because they dislike your unpleasant dogmatism and spiritual pride.

Don't prescribe to God how He should answer your prayers for your partner. You may think that hearing a particular preacher will be the answer. How wrong we often are. Let us not try to manipulate God. He will do His work in His way and in His time.

Don't expect God to honour you in your home if you are disobedient to God's plan for your role in the family. If your behaviour is no different from that of your unconverted neighbour, why should your unsaved spouse believe what you believe?

Christians living with an unsaved partner need God's wisdom. Allow the beauty of Jesus to be seen in you without giving in on crucial issues. Love your partner, seek his or her well-being, honour God in your home, pray and quietly beseech God for the salvation of your family. Then step back and watch Him at work!

Is there hope for the guilty partner?

Let's examine this important question. I realise that a partner sometimes walks out because of problems that have accumulated over a period of time, not because he or she is the sole cause of all the trouble. Both may share the blame. But while this is true, all too often one partner is not willing to keep the vows, maintain the marriage or get help to heal a hurting relationship. They may allow their own selfish interests to predominate in the marriage. They therefore become the cause of the breakdown.

What happens if such a person finally becomes a Christian? What do they do about their divorced partner? In fact, what do they do with their lives? Often real regret follows such behaviour. Sin always complicates our lives and becoming a Christian does not always 'uncomplicate' things. There is often still a price to pay. Take Stuart and Mary as an example.

For the first few years of his marriage, Stuart was a model husband. Mary was his ideal of womanhood. Their courtship and marriage were the stuff dreams are made of. They were reasonably affluent and purchased a small renovated cottage. Every item of furniture they bought together had a history of searching and bargaining, repainting and being proudly put into place. The two babies were cute, well cared for and loved. Life settled into a comfortable routine.

Stuart did not plan to meet Suzi. She moved into the office as a new computer programmer. He could not understand his attraction to her. Confusion, shyness and guilt gradually gave way to friendliness. He began to feel comfortable with her. Shared jokes increased their familiarity and he grew increasingly aware of her attractiveness.

At first he denied that anything was happening. But slowly his habits began to change. He became terribly self-conscious in her presence, tried to impress her and became withdrawn and irritable at home. This led to arguments and tension he and Mary had never known before. She was no longer attractive to him. Their sex life dwindled. She became a nuisance, as did the children. He was filled with confusion as his feelings vacillated between guilt and remorse, anger and frustration.

Finally the affair with Suzi began. Stuart and Suzi tried to rationalise their behaviour by 'being honest' as so many adulterers do. It was almost as if honesty about their actions and intentions would expunge their guilt. The inevitable divorce followed, and Stuart set up a new home with Suzi while they made plans to marry.

Just as Stuart had not bargained on an affair with Suzi, he had not considered the possibility of the emotional fire dying. But it did. They began to squabble. She was always in tears and his guilt increased. He insulted her until neither could take it any more and they went their separate ways.

Stuart was alone. From a well-kept, homely cottage with a warm, responsive wife by his side at night, lovely children, the smell of home cooking, he was left with a sparsely furnished flat, a broken romance, a depleted bank account and impaired performance at work. He was filled with guilt, remorse, regret and contempt for himself.

The contact with his children only underscored all he had lost. He decided to talk to Mary. Perhaps there was still hope. His despair knew no bounds when he discovered that she was seeing someone else and was no longer interested in him.

Stuart worked with a Christian friend. Through this contact, he saw a Christian counsellor to find a way forward out of his despair. He longed for a meaningful life and a way to live with himself again. As the guilty party, responsible for the break-up of his marriage, Stuart had to face the issues of guilt, forgiveness, restitution, proving himself, self-pity, spiritual growth and remarriage.

Guilt

The first thing Stuart needed to realise was the enormity of the sin he had committed. Not merely against Mary, the children, Suzi and himself, but against God. He had broken the seventh commandment.

Remorse and regrets, based on the selfish awareness of what he had lost, were not enough. He needed to recognise that he had sinned against God. God does not allow sin to go unpunished.

Forgiveness

Stuart needed to be told that, great as his sin was, God forgives sin. Jesus Christ, the Son of God, bore the punishment on his behalf. The torment of guilt drove Judas Iscariot to suicide. But God has opened a way for sinners to find peace and a clean conscience. We are forgiven as we yield our lives to Jesus Christ who shed His blood to atone for our sins. The salvation God has provided for us in Jesus Christ washes away the stain and guilt of the worst sin we could commit. This means that, horrible though your action may have been in breaking up your marriage, the guilt of your sin can be forgiven.

Forgiveness of our sins, especially that of breaking up a home, does not cancel the consequences of our actions. Although you become a Christian with a new nature, you may still have to live with the fact that you have broken the hearts of others and scarred their lives. It therefore behoves the guilty party who has become a Christian to remember with great solemnity the depths of their offence, the greatness of the hurt they have caused and the immensity of Christ's action on the cross to provide their forgiveness.

Stuart needed great humility and an awareness that time was needed to establish his credibility as a Christian. But no matter how great our sin may be, we find hope if we respond to God's invitation to come to Christ for forgiveness.

May I ask if you have found forgiveness? It is no good living with remorse, depression and despair. Forgiveness and a new life are available if you come to Christ and receive Him as your personal Saviour. You may not be able to undo the harm you have done, but you can spend the rest of your life proving how repentant you are by living for God in a positive and constructive manner with the help of the Holy Spirit.

Restitution

As the guilty party you may need to make amends to your family. Do not allow guilt and remorse to rush you into a sensitive situation. Stuart needed to back off and leave matters alone. Moving in and out of their lives only increased the hurt and confusion. Both your ex-spouse and the children need time to find equilibrium. They may just have found some sort of balance and your sudden appearance could upset the fragile balance.

If there is a chance of reconciliation, work slowly with the guidance of a marriage counsellor. A dreadful thing has happened in your lives and a pep talk or spiritual band-aid will not help. Problems have to be faced and resolved and hurts may take a long time to heal. But do not be impatient. Wait and pray.

Prove yourself

If your guilt has included abuse, addiction or unfaithfulness, do not expect your spouse to take you back simply because you claim to have changed. If you have had a true Christian experience, you will realise the need to prove your bona fides.

Be prepared to keep a low profile. Prove that you are a Christian not simply to get your family back, but because it is a matter of conviction. Concentrate on building your relationship with Christ. Be willing to be humble and to assist your church in even menial things. Establish a reputation as a genuine Christian. Even if you never win your family back, be grateful for God's forgiveness, build a new life and prove yourself as a true believer.

Self-pity

Do not allow your regret and loneliness to degenerate into self-pity. If your spouse does not want you, your children are not keen to spend time with you and your other relationships have failed, remember that this is what you deserved!

Proverbs 11:29 (NKJV) says:

> He who troubles his own house will inherit the wind,
> And the fool will be servant to the wise of heart.

In Galatians 6:7 (NKJV) we read:

> Do not be deceived, God is not mocked; for whatever a man sows, that he will also reap.

The fact that you have been forgiven does not mean that the consequences of your actions are negated. Do not give in to self-pity and bitterness, especially if your spouse remarries and your children begin to call their step-parent 'mummy' or 'daddy'. It is your fault. Bow before

God, accept the consequences, thank Him for forgiving you and get on with your life.

Spiritual growth

The only way to cope with your own changing emotions, once you have accepted Christ and are facing the reality of a lost family, is to make sure that your relationship with God is real and growing. Find a church that will help you, where God's Word is expounded faithfully and systematically.

Approach Christian people and make new friends among them. Seek help to read the Bible in a way that is meaningful. Discover the true meaning of prayer. Get involved in Christian activity and share your faith with others.

As you grow in your awareness of eternal issues, you will become more concerned about the spiritual well-being of the family you have left behind. Pray for them. Use every opportunity to do good to them without appearing to be a pushy Bible-puncher. They may not know you in your role as a Christian and it may appear to be a ploy to get them back. Be sincere and sensitive and concentrate on your spiritual growth and development.

Remarriage

Can you, as the guilty partner, ever enter another marriage? A cautious, thoughtful approach is needed in thinking through this issue.

It is inappropriate for the guilty spouse who comes to repentance and Christian conversion to rush into another marriage. Every effort must be made to seek reconciliation if that is at all possible. In addition, a superhuman effort is needed to make restitution for the hurt, damage and loss the family has suffered. This must be done with caution and sensitivity.

If, after a suitable period, all efforts to re-establish the family unit with the help of counsellors and pastors fail or your ex-spouse remarries, that chapter of your life must be closed. Having repented, made every effort at restitution and established your spiritual bona fides, you may plan with great carefulness and humility to marry again.

Some people may think it unfair for a partner who has caused so much damage and hurt to be allowed to remarry and become a respectable member of the church. But God's forgiveness is immense and makes us new creatures.

> Therefore, if anyone is in Christ, he is a new creation; old things have passed away; behold, all things have become new (2 Cor. 5:17, NKJV).

God's magnificent act of grace restores us to fellowship with Him. Along with millions of other sinners of the worst kind, the adulterer and divorcee may find new hope and new life.

I want to stress that I am talking about genuine conversion, not empty, hypocritical claims. A church minister who is aware of the issues involved will want to do a great deal of counselling before allowing a guilty person a Christian remarriage. If the claim to be a Christian is superficial or there has been no track record of a true repentance and humility before God, or if there is no genuine sorrow for past behaviour, to grant such a person a Christian marriage would be to perpetuate the abuse Jesus condemned (Matt. 19:1-8).

A further consideration to bear in mind in thinking through this issue is the fact that, if the guilty party becomes a Christian, he or she may only marry a Christian (1 Cor. 7:39; 2 Cor. 6:14-18). On the other hand, if the ex-spouse to whom the repentant partner wants to be reconciled is resolutely opposed to Christianity, even though they were the offended party, an added complication arises.

When all is said and done, we have to acknowledge the paucity of our wisdom. We attempt to deal with each case on its own merit according to Scripture and our limited understanding. One thing is true – Jesus Christ, the Son of God, forgives our sins. Our hope lies in Him.

Chapter 14

Domestic violence and the Christian

We now approach a subject of great sensitivity. The problem of domestic violence is receiving increasing media coverage as the abuse of women and children is given the attention it deserves. The horrendous trauma of this crime is cause for great concern, and the complexities, humiliation and pain are great.

To date not much has been written about this difficult subject by Christians. Most books dealing with marriage problems from a Christian perspective seem either to ignore or skip over the problem of domestic violence. Some authors seem to take the reader up to a point and leave them to work things out for themselves.

In my opinion, there are many Christians who need more specific help in thinking things through and coming to a decision. However, this is a sensitive subject and I acknowledge that there are no easy answers.

What does the Bible say?

One of the problems Christians face is that the Bible itself does not appear to make any comment about this sin. Domestic violence, i.e. a husband beating his wife, is referred to in Scripture only once. We will note the oblique reference in Malachi 2:16 later. There are hints that slaves were beaten, but not wives. Why is the Scripture silent on this point?

In his book *Hebrew Marriage*, David Mace shows how the status of a Hebrew woman was completely bound up with her place in the home. In ancient Semitic nations, there were often two kinds of women in the home: a female slave and the lawful wife. The female slave was treated as the owner's property and may even have been beaten (Exod. 21:20-21). Despite this, she could rise considerably in status (vv. 1-11).

The wife, however, was not secured by purchase, as a slave might be, but by negotiation with her parents and the presentation of a compensation-gift. The wife was not a slave or a chattel but a person of status. She had rights and privileges and could appeal to her family for help when these were denied her. Note for instance the intervention of the girl's family in a domestic dispute in Deuteronomy 22:13-19. She usually had her own tent, could possess property and might own servants. Proverbs 31 describes the business enterprises she could undertake, the love and respect she commanded from her family and her devotion to them.

Mace maintains that the only sense in which the wife could be viewed as her husband's property was in regard to her sexuality. This was the exclusive and inviolable property of her husband. The laws relating to the violation of women, adultery and divorce were based on this notion.

The Old Testament therefore recognised the wife as a person of worth. She was her husband's property only in the sense that her sexuality was regarded as part of his inviolable goods. The evil practice of quick divorce that developed in Israel disposed only of the wife's sexuality. Her husband had no right to injure her, have her killed or sell her as he could a slave. She was subject to him, took his name, passed from the authority of her father to that of her husband, honoured him as head of the home and entered into an intimate personal relationship with him, but her husband did not own her.

This has implications for us today. Many husbands excuse their wife beating on the grounds that 'she is my wife'. They imply that she is a possession that they can treat as they please.

In Old Testament times the wife performed three basic functions within the marriage relationship. She was a source of sexual pleasure to her husband, a means of obtaining progeny, but, most importantly, she was his companion. She entered a legal agreement with her husband to play this role, but he in turn had obligations towards her.

In this context it was unthinkable for a wife to be the object of violence. It was not part of ancient biblical thinking or culture. She could be unfairly disposed of as a wife, but if she was so much as slandered against, her husband was punished severely (Deut. 22:13-19).

Family violence was not the norm in Israel although, sinful human nature being what it is, violence must occasionally have taken place. So foreign was it to Hebrew thinking that it was not even mentioned in Israel's legislation.

There is even less to go on in the New Testament. Our Lord rebuked the Pharisees because their unbiblical application of Moses' law pertaining to divorce amounted to abuse, but there is no mention of domestic violence. 1 Corinthians 7 deals with the reaction of an unbelieving partner who leaves his believing wife and 1 Peter 3 addresses a wife whose unbelieving partner will not listen to the gospel, but violence is not mentioned.

Where, then, do we find biblical guidelines to deal with the problem of violence in the home? What should the Christian response be to this problem? I believe the answer lies in the sixth command: 'You shall not murder' (Exod. 20:13).

In fact in the New Testament violence is attributed to Satan. He is the source of this crime. Jesus called Satan a murderer and a creature of violence from the beginning (John 8:44).

As we saw when we referred to domestic violence in chapter five, the Ten Commandments operate on the principle of synecdoche. Jesus taught that if the greater sin is forbidden, it follows that lesser related sins are forbidden too (Matt. 5:17-48). Therefore if murder was forbidden, then *all forms of injury were also forbidden*.

The New Testament confirms the biblical teaching that malice, the mainspring of violence, should not have a foothold in the life of a Christian. It is plain that Matthew 5:21-22 that the sixth commandment covers all forms of violence, hatred and aggression. Paul underscores this:

Do not take revenge, my friends, but leave room for God's wrath, for it is written, 'It is mine to avenge; I will repay,' says the Lord (Rom. 12:19).

Get rid of all bitterness, rage and anger, brawling and slander, along with every form of malice. Be kind and compassionate to one another, forgiving each other, just as in Christ God forgave you (Eph. 4:31-32).

John, the apostle of love, brought the same message:

Anyone who hates his brother is a murderer, and you know that no murderer has eternal life in him (1 John 3:15).

Hatred, aggression and murder are synonymous in New Testament thinking.

Malachi 2:16 is a clear statement of God's opposition not only to divorce but to family violence, much as we know it today:

'I hate divorce,' says the LORD God of Israel, 'and I hate a man's covering himself with violence as well as with his garment,' says the LORD Almighty.

The footnote in the NIV says 'Or *his wife*'. The verse could therefore read:

'I hate a man's covering *his wife* with violence as well as with his garment,' says the LORD Almighty.

Covering with a garment is a reference to the sexual act. Thus the verse is a reference to domestic violence followed by sex. Violence breaks the marriage covenant, denounces the vows 'to have and to hold ... till death parts us' and negates the rules of marriage (Mal. 2:14). A normal marriage cannot exist under these circumstances.

What must a victimised spouse do? There can be only one answer: she must leave. If the guilty partner's behaviour does not change and reconciliation is impossible, she must actively seek a divorce because the marriage has become a mockery. Life and limb are endangered, her dignity and self-worth are being destroyed and the vital element of respect has been lost. There is no longer any basis for the marriage because the covenant conditions have been broken and dishonoured.

A major decision

To say a woman living in these circumstances should leave is one thing; for her actually to do so is another. The mere logistics of leaving may be too much to bear. Where will she go with her children? How will she live without money? What about the children's schooling? These and a myriad other considerations cause battered women to lose heart.

But there is another and more subtle development that prevents a woman from leaving. When a man beats a wife, he is making a statement about her worth, not only by the violent act itself but by the verbal barrage of abuse that often accompanies it. Women are often told that they were the cause of the beating, that they provoked their husbands, that they in fact *deserve* it. Sadly, many women come to believe they do in some way deserve it!

Men often become more and more violent as time passes. They react to any little thing that they perceive is a challenge to their authority in the home. Fear becomes an integral part of daily life. If the wife puts up with the violence, it is tacit acceptance of this evaluation of her as a person. The relationship deteriorates. The man often threatens to throw her out of the house. He may taunt her saying that he will not give her the children or support her. Her feelings of insecurity and vulnerability increase.

In their study *Violence Against Wives*, Dobash and Dobash point out that each successive violent episode leaves the woman with less hope and self-esteem. Fear increases and the man becomes accustomed to hitting his wife. He finally ceases to see himself as doing anything wrong. As the situation deteriorates, the woman feels more and more isolated and hopeless.

Once this stage is reached, it is very difficult to leave. I urge you not to accept this lifestyle; do not accept this evaluation of yourself. If you are a Christian, you really do not have the right to live in this situation because it is a caricature of marriage and relationships. For one partner to drag the marriage covenant down into the dust in this way is entirely wrong and must be resisted.

Support

Support from outside sources is very important. The experience of most people today is that neighbours and friends seldom get involved when family violence is being perpetrated. However, it was not always so. Case histories exist of communities so disapproving of the wife-beater that he had to move to escape public contempt.

Unfortunately now the community seldom gets involved. Instead they call the police. In other words, it is no longer a community problem but has become a state problem.

It is satisfying to notice that the courts are now becoming far more active in cases of domestic violence. The new culture of personal rights has at least had the effect of the law taking the abuse of women and children more seriously. Although we could all quote examples of terrible family violence, I want to draw your attention to one such case because the argument for the defence in this case made a surprising assessment of the value of the wife and children.

The man accused was found guilty of the most horrendous abuse which included sodomising his wife on the kitchen table, bashing her head against the wall, hitting her and threatening to hang her up and beat her with a spade. On the same day he tied a dog leash around her neck and forced her to crawl around the house and eat dog food. When he was sentenced to eleven years' imprisonment, his lawyer argued in mitigation that he was high on drugs, got into a domestic quarrel and was 'not a danger to society'!

The assessment of his lawyer was that his wife and children were not 'society'. This unfortunately has been the case all too often in the past. If the man had been arrested for assaulting a woman on the street, he would be summarily dealt with by the courts. He has no right to assault another human being. But the reluctance of the authorities in the past to take action in cases of the woman being assaulted by her husband in her home has at its root the same idea as the defence lawyer quoted above. Outside the home, she is protected by law but somehow inside the home she ceases to be a normal citizen and becomes a 'wife' which by implication means a possession and therefore fair game for assault. Likewise, if her husband had to assault another woman, he would be considered a criminal. But because she is his wife, his actions are not considered criminal but domestic.

The sad thing is that many Christians who should be enlightened and thinking people are unable to see the wood for the trees when it comes to domestic violence. I have had to deal with terrible cases of domestic violence where in seeking spiritual guidance, the battered wife who is a Christian has been told to go back into that very situation of danger and emotional destruction and 'submit'. In doing so, she is told, God will bless her and vindicate her. Yet if she was assaulted at a bus stop by a stranger, those same friends would in all likelihood encourage her to lay a charge.

Fortunately the judge in the case referred to above said, in sentencing the husband:

> You had absolutely no respect for your wife's bodily integrity. This was degradation in the highest degree. It is shocking and horrifying that a grown-up man can treat his own wife like this (*Argus*, 11 August 1994).

I understand how hopeless and demotivated women can become in these circumstances. Sometimes it seems better to live in such a way that they negotiate minimum violence levels rather than face the seemingly impossible task of leaving and starting a new life for themselves.

But I repeat, with understanding and compassion, that it is essential to leave. It is indeed a major decision.

Leaving and returning
Why do women put up with violence? Why don't they leave? They answer is that many do leave – but often not with the intention of this being permanent. All sorts of dynamics come into play in a sad situation of domestic violence.

Promises
Dobash and Dobash make the following comment:

> As has been noted already, the woman initially believes that the violence will not continue and that her husband will reform. At this point she may go to her parents' house for a few hours or a few days in order to emphasise her

objections to such treatment and to try to hasten what she believes will be the process of reform by letting her husband see what it would be like without her presence, her affection, her domestic work, and, in many cases, her financial support or contributions. The intention is not to leave the relationship permanently but to try to gain some form of redress and to change the relationship by removing the violence from it. At this very early stage the sequence of events is almost always the same: the woman's husband goes after her, apologises for hitting her, acknowledges the error of his ways, promises that it will never happen again, reaffirms his affection for her, and pleads with her to come home.

Women often return to their violent homes because they believe their husbands' promises. But unless the problems have been permanently resolved, the reconciliation will be superficial and meaningless. Women do not need promises but an inner power or dynamic to bring about change. We will talk about this dynamic later.

Children

Promises are not the only thing that induce women to return to violent homes. Often women stay for the sake of the children. They believe that the children need their father and must not be traumatised by a broken home. While it is true that children need their fathers, they do not need to live with fathers who abuse their mother. The woman, however, feels responsible for the children because their physical care rests almost exclusively with her.

They also fear the possibility of violence spilling over to the children. Ironically, most women will draw a line at this point and make some plan to leave with the children.

In fact, sometimes the fear of the children learning violence from their own fathers plays a major role in helping battered women to leave. On the other hand, if there is no way they can care adequately for the children's material needs by themselves, women may feel trapped and unable to leave.

No excuse
Let me say at this point that there is never any excuse for violence of this nature in a Christian home. A man who claims to be a Christian and yet freely abuses his family either verbally or physically is an utter contradiction in terms. It cannot be. Christians are meant to be Christlike in all their dealings with each other. I know that we aren't perfect. We all make mistakes and often say things we regret. But for a Christian to be guilty of abuse in the home goes way beyond 'making mistakes'. It is downright sinful and evil. Any person who claims to be a follower of Jesus and yet is able to perpetrate violence is deluded.

I am aware of how sensitive this issue is. I have no wish to see families broken by divorce. But neither do I wish to see the devastation brought about by meaningless reconciliation and the secret covering up of violence. The tensions, anxieties and depressions that follow present the children with a terrible model of marriage.

Someone has to take action. No one can tell you exactly what to do. I certainly do not have all the answers. Some victims will have more options than others, but the situation should not be allowed to continue.

Taking action
For a woman caught up in these circumstances the problem of fear arises at this point – fear of the physical

consequences of leaving and fear of the unknown. Where must she go? How will she cope financially? What will she do? Friends and the police are reluctant to get involved and the woman is often left defenceless. Let us look at practical ways of dealing with this situation.

Decide against violence

Firstly, *make a mental decision*, an act of the will, that you will no longer live with violence. This may be a very difficult bridge to cross but you must do it. Violence is wrong. It is doubly wrong if the children become part of the abuse. Their only hope lies with you. You must pray for God's help, then explore every avenue to get intervention in the home. Do not put up with it. You must move out.

Biblical action

Secondly, remember that by moving out, *you are not doing anything unbiblical*. Many Christians caught up in family violence are reluctant to make the move because they feel they are dishonouring the marriage vows they made to God. You must remember that marriage before God and vows exchanged in His presence do not entail violence. That is not what 'for better or for worse' means. 'For better or for worse' refers to the ordinary ups and downs of life – not ongoing destructive abuse.

It is possible for marriage vows to be broken in more ways than one. It is not only marital unfaithfulness that breaks the vows but also the failure to love and cherish. Read again my comments in the earlier part of this chapter about the sixth commandment. No one has the right to injure you – not even your husband. It is a flagrant breach of the marriage vows.

Promises

Thirdly, *do not give in to promises.* If you do move out, your husband will in all likelihood make all sorts of promises to get you back. You simply must not believe him. You need to know that once a cycle of violence has begun in the home, it is not likely to stop of its own accord. Something happens to the relationship once a physical blow has been struck. The guilty partner must get counselling help. There must be genuine repentance. No matter how much you love him or the children pine for him, you must not go back simply on the basis of his promises.

'But you are my wife'

Fourthly, *do not give in to the argument 'But you are my wife'.* No matter what has transpired, remember that you do not own each other. He does not own you. For Christians marriage is a voluntary act based on trust and the goodwill of your partner. He does not own your mind, your opinions or your convictions. The only thing that he can lay exclusive claim to is your sexuality. But even that is forfeited if he doesn't keep his vows to love and cherish you.

If the relationship is normal, you will want to support your partner in all things and be part of all that happens in his life, and he in yours. But when there is violence, the marriage *is not normal.* To forgive too easily, to overlook it quickly, to trivialise it or play it down is to make a big mistake. You are indeed his wife – a treasured and precious possession. But only God owns you totally (1 Cor. 6:19-20). Do not be bullied into thinking otherwise.

Separation

Fifthly, remember that by leaving *you are not necessarily ending the marriage*. You are making a very important statement. You are saying: 'I refuse to live like this any longer.' You are sending him a clear signal that a line has been crossed which you will not tolerate.

The sooner you do it, the better. The longer you leave it, the more difficult and complicated it becomes. If you are newly married and your husband has been abusive, do not make the mistake of thinking that becoming pregnant will, in some way, save your marriage. It may work for a short while but will not solve the problem. Rather, the first time he is ever violent with you – leave. Draw the line early in your marriage. That means that there is a better chance to working things out.

Leaving means that your husband has to assess whether he really wants you or not. Do not be conned into feeling sorry for him when he presents himself as the aggrieved party, the miserable skunk who has wrecked your life but cannot live without you, or by his suicide threats. These are old ploys, designed to melt your opposition or panic you into coming back. *Don't do it*.

Instead, calmly and quietly insist on counselling. Inform him that you will not go back on his conditions. *You* must lay down the conditions. These should include at least two things. Firstly, he should submit himself to biblical confrontation and counselling, and secondly, there should be a break of some time for him to establish a spiritual track record.

If you do go back and violence recurs, leave permanently. You are wasting your time. Leave him for God to deal with and make a new life for yourself. Remember that your leaving is not primarily in order to divorce but rather to give your marriage a chance by taking a stand against what is wrong.

Seek help

Sixthly, sometimes a violent man will follow you with his violence, no matter where you go. I have no answer for every situation but I want to stress as strongly as I can that, if these are your circumstances, *you must get help to restrain him.* You will need to fight a great deal of fear, but wife and children beaters are bullies and need to be bullied back – not in revenge, but rather through the channels the law gives you. You must find a way to stand up to him.

This was graphically illustrated by a woman interviewed by a news reporter doing a story on wife battering. She told of horrific beatings of her and her children with little sympathy from the community where she lived. She tried on numerous occasions to escape. This is what she said:

> After moving house more than five times in a bid to stop John finding out where she lived, Elizabeth decided to stop running and fight back.
>
> 'I had to stop moving around for my children's sake. They attended three different schools in one year.
>
> 'Both of them told me that if their father turned up again they would protect me. They said they weren't scared of him any more and that's when I realised I shouldn't be scared either.'
>
> When John appeared on her doorstep three months ago, Elizabeth confronted him and told him she refused to bear the brunt of his frustrations any longer.

'He got such a big fright, he didn't know what to say. My sons also told him that they wouldn't let him hit me any more.

'He's such a big bully. He just turned around and left and we've never seen him again.

'I should have realised long ago that all I had to do was tell him that I wouldn't let him hit me again.'

(*Weekend Argus*, 13 June 1987)

- If you have family or friends who are willing to take you in, grasp the opportunity. Those close to you may not want to be involved with your marital strife and may be reluctant to shelter you, but if you are fortunate enough to have a place to go, use it.

- Do not hesitate to lay a criminal charge of assault against your husband if necessary. You may feel guilty about it, but everybody's hands are tied, especially the police, unless you do. Violent men do not believe that their wives will take action and are often shocked when they do. Wives are sometimes intimidated by their partners' threats to kill themselves and their children. Only by laying a charge will you prove to your husband that you are serious about resisting his violent behaviour.

- Ask for protection from the police. See a lawyer immediately and get an interdict to stop your husband from seeing you or the children until a divorce settlement has been reached. The police can only act on an interdict.

- Changes are taking place all over the world today in the laws affecting family abuse. Find out, if you can, what these changes are.

- Try to find a safe place. It may not be the ideal place, but put up with it until the crisis is over. In this regard, try to establish which would be the best organisation to contact in your town. Keep their local telephone number handy.

Fortunately this type of extreme violence is not everybody's experience. Extreme cases need extreme action. But in the more frequent cases of violence, a wife needs to take a stand as quickly and as effectively as possible.

I remind you again that you are not breaking any biblical rules by taking action. On the contrary, by remaining in the situation and exposing yourself and your children to an ongoing situation of violence, you could in fact be doing more spiritual harm than good. Remember that Scripture tells us: 'If it is possible, as far as it depends on you, live at peace with everyone' (Rom. 12:18).

God's desire is for us to live at peace with everyone – including our spouses. However, because we are fallen and sinful, it is inevitable that there will be conflict. Our Lord has given us rules for resolving conflict, but if everything fails, what do we do? What if the conflict turns to violence?

Remove yourself to a place where you can live at peace. Paul says, 'as far as it depends on you, live at peace with everyone'. Have you done all you could, have you tried, pleaded, prayed – gone the second mile? Then you can do no more. You can only do what is possible, not what is impossible. You are free to leave. In fact, you must leave. As I have already indicated, as a Christian woman you have no right to remain in a wicked, demeaning situation.

Ignore the advice of well-meaning friends and family who, in their ignorance of Bible teaching, will tell you to pray, submit and keep the family together. Although this is important, God's law is more important: 'You shall not commit murder'.

Domestic violence not only breaks this commandment in its most basic form, but many other things are 'murdered' too. Your self-image and self-respect, your Christian witness, the children's view of marriage, their emotional well-being and the right to grow up in safety and peace are all affected. Think of these things and ask God to guide you in planning your withdrawal from the home.

Withdrawing from a violent home can be the only immediate Christian response. I know that all victims do not experience the same kind of violence and fear, but it is my conviction that a Christian should not tolerate violence in the home.

Don't give in to fear

Seventhly, your withdrawal from your home and the subsequent threat of a total marriage breakdown can have a devastating emotional effect on you and the children. As a result there may be the temptation to give in to panic. This very panic has often driven women and children back again into a home of violence and terror because the fear of the familiar sometimes outweighs the fear of the unknown. *But don't give in to fear*.

You may be really frightened and anxious of the financial consequences of leaving. But before going back into the violent situation you need to sit down with a pastor, counsellor or trusted friend and begin to plan your life. While the reconciliation process is being investigated or divorce proceedings are instigated, you must fight the temptation to become depressed or demotivated. You need friends and support.

One of the things you will need to do is to get back into the workplace. This alone may present many problems. You may have small children to care for and provision will have to be made for them. You may not have any job skills or your training may be out of date. If you do find a job and your estranged husband is not assisting you financially, you may find it very difficult to make ends meet. On the other hand you may have to depend on the kindness of family and friends for a while until you get yourself sorted out.

Summary

All these things may present themselves as difficulties and discouragements. But don't give up. Try to get a job, try to get your family organised, try to improve your skills. Don't simply sit back and sink into despair.

When your husband sees that you mean business and are surrounded by supportive friends, he will usually back off. At the same time, I know only too well how unpredictable human nature can be. You may be constantly harassed by him. If you are caught up in this situation, make sure that you have legal and police protection, and the backing of as many friends as possible. You should have a support group praying for you.

God is great and merciful. He is not unmindful of your needs. He knows your fears, anxieties, financial hardship and emotional stress. He looks with love and pity on your children. It is not beyond His power to care for all of you.

Nor is it outside His power to do something new in your husband's heart.

I said earlier that what is needed is a new inner dynamic. That dynamic is the new birth, the new nature. Once your partner has the new nature which God imparts to all who come to Christ, all change is possible. For all who come to Christ, there is the wonderful experience of being indwelt by the Holy Spirit. He brings the very power of God into our hearts – and even the hardest of hearts can be transformed by His grace.

These are the things that you and your friends should be praying for while you are adapting to a new set of circumstances. Do not fear. Remember God. Remember His power. Remember His promises. Here is one you can cling to by faith:

> But now, this is what the LORD says –
>> he who created you, O Jacob,
>> he who formed you, O Israel:
> 'Fear not, for I have redeemed you;
> I have summoned you by name; you are mine.
> When you pass through the waters,
>> I will be with you;
> And when you pass through the rivers,
>> they will not sweep over you.
> When you walk through the fire,
>> you will not be burned;
>> the flames will not set you ablaze.'
> (Isa. 43:1-2)

Chapter 15

Putting your marriage
into perspective

Divorce is to be avoided if at all possible. Although it is a resort, it is always the very last resort. Often divorces take place that were not necessary. The response to the crisis in the home may be wrong, unwise and sinful in God's eyes. Wise counsel, some clarity of thought and a little bit of perspective might have avoided the sadness and trauma that always accompanies the breakup of a marriage.

When a marriage breaks up, a home breaks up as well. In fact, there a number of things that 'break up' when a marriage fails. Dreams, hopes and aspirations that disintegrate. Children lose their sense of security when the familiar structures of family life disappear. Emotions, a sense of significance and purpose, identity and direction disintegrates with the disintegrating relationship. If it is at all possible, don't get divorced.

Sometimes the accumulated hurt is so great that it is hard to make a proper assessment. Let's take a few minutes to place your marriage in perspective. You may be facing a divorce right now and it may not be of your own making. You may well have no control over it. Much as you hate and fear the prospect, you know it is going to happen because your partner wants out. If, however, the divorce is going through because neither of you has had help to get perspective, this chapter may help to initiate a new round of discussions and negotiations. Don't be too cynical or downhearted. Give it a try.

Let's try to get some perspective on your marriage problems by asking some important questions.

Is the problem really unresolvable?

Problems can usually be resolved unless one party refuses to play their part. If one of the parties is stubborn, proud, intransigent and determined to end the relationship, there is nothing the other can do about it. But is that really the situation in your case? Think about it for a moment.

What are the things that have brought you to this point where a divorce is imminent? Were they really big things? Or were they an accumulation of small and petty things that were never resolved? When small things are not resolved, they develop into big issues and the two people grow further apart.

One of the first things to go is communication. If you stop talking to each other, nothing can ever be sorted out. I know that the main complaint of wives is that their husbands don't talk to them. That is a real problem and it needs to be dealt with, but that is not what I am referring to here. I am asking whether the problems that have led to a divorce action have ever really been discussed.

Think of all the hours and days which could have been happy times together but have been wasted because of pettiness and sulking. Your life is not so long that you can afford to waste time on pettiness. Pettiness is a form of selfishness and pride. Our enemy the devil knows exactly

220

how to use this human weakness to drive a wedge between two people so that a happy and potentially wonderful home becomes nothing more than another miserable statistic. Don't let it happen. Don't let pettiness rob you of each other, or your children of their home and parents. It's simply not worth it.

I have already referred to the violent terrorist attack that took place in my church in July 1993. I also referred to the way it caused us all to reflect on life and its uncertainty. I posed the question about what would matter to you if you knew that you only had five minutes to live.

I have often thought that, in that situation, I wouldn't care who had won the last argument. Nor would I care what others thought of me. I wouldn't care about the million silly little things that annoy me in the course of an ordinary day.

What would I care about? Apart from my relationship with God, I would care about when last I took my wife in my arms, kissed her and told her I loved her. I would care about letting her know how much I appreciated her and all she has to put up with living with me. I would care about thanking her for the children she has borne me and her devotion to me and to them. I would care about when last I put my arms around my sons and told them how proud I am of them, and of my daughter. I would wonder when last I told her she was just like her pretty mother and she made my heart glad.

What about you? Is your problem really unresolvable? Has there been a real and honest attempt at reaching a solution?

This leads to my second question.

Have you sought true Christian counselling?

So often when a husband announces he is leaving, the distraught wife goes to the doctor for help. She wants an explanation of the situation as if what was happening were a medical problem. Often she does this because, in her panic, she needs someone to talk to. She wants someone to put things right – to reverse what is happening.

She then may do the rounds to friends and psychiatrists. She may even persuade her husband to see a psychiatrist or a family counsellor – all to no avail, because the problem is usually not medical or psychological but spiritual. It is rebellion against God's revealed order for human relationships. There is only one book that deals with that problem and that is the Bible.

For many people, however, seeing a Christian counsellor is a last resort. Often the counsellor then has a mammoth task of first clearing all the useless advice that has accumulated, recognising and dealing with the pain, and at the same time laying down basic biblical principles as foundations on which to build a pastoral counselling programme.

A few comments need to be made about this. The first is that even biblical counselling cannot reverse the process of divorce if the other party is not interested. Both partners must have a genuine desire to seek solutions before help can be given.

A second comment is that often even those who present themselves as Christian counsellors do not really understand the dynamics of the human heart. Instead of giving biblical counsel they may complicate matters by offering pious platitudes and advice based on previous prejudices. It is so important to get expert, spiritual, mature biblical advice. Have you done that?

A biblical counsellor will analyse your problems biblically. He will point to action that is biblical and will work if followed because it is based on God's Word. Obedience to God's Word brings positive results. There may be a lot of hard work to do and things may not be resolved overnight, but a commitment to the Word of God is the true and only way to save your marriage.

Have you recognised the differences between men and women?

Sometimes we have unrealistic expectations of each other. We don't realise that men and women often respond to life differently. What a man deems important, a woman does not always see as important and vice versa. I can do no better than to recommend that you obtain a copy of James Dobson's excellent book entitled *Straight Talk*. He describes in his own inimitable way the things that make men and women tick:

> Anyone who doubts that males and females are unique should observe how they approach a game of Ping Pong or Monopoly or dominoes or horseshoes or volleyball or tennis. Women often use the event as an excuse for fellowship and pleasant conversation. For men, the name of the game is *conquest*. Even if the setting is a friendly social gathering in the host's backyard, the beads of sweat on each man's forehead reveal his passion to win. This aggressive competitiveness has been attributed to cultural influences. I don't believe it. As Richard Restak said, 'At a birthday party for five-year-olds, it's not usually the girls who pull hair, throw punches, or smear each other with food.'

> Males and females apparently differ in the manner by which they develop self-esteem. Men draw the necessary

evidence of their worthiness primarily from their jobs – from being respected in business, profession or craft. Women, however, *especially those who are homemakers*, depend primarily on the romantic relationship with their husbands for ego support. This explains why the emotional content of a marriage is often of greater significance to women than men and why tokens of affection are appreciated more by wives, who obtain esteem from these expressions of love and generosity (p. 153).

Read this book before you go through with your divorce. It may just throw new light on your problems and save you a lot of heartache.

The point I am making is that often our hurts are caused unnecessarily because we have not taken into account sufficiently the differences God has built into us. If we understand that and make allowances for it with graciousness and humility, many divorce actions will be scrapped.

Have you thought about the seriousness of divorce?

This may sound very obvious, but have you? You may not realise how many people go through with a divorce only to live with regrets for the rest of their lives. Divorce affects not only the two of you but a whole circle of people – both family and friends. The emotional devastation referred to in the first chapter cannot be emphasised enough. It is always more difficult to put emotions back together again than to heal broken bones.

Two selfish adults fighting over trivia may take no thought for what is happening in the hearts and minds of their children. These children are watching the only world they know slowly falling apart. Loyalties are stretched to breaking point, confusion and pain set in that can affect them into their adult years.

What is even worse is that the only real model they have of how men and women should relate to each other is you! If you fail, where do they go? How will they ever conduct a happy marriage? If abuse, bickering and strained relationships is all they know, that may well become the norm for them, the model they themselves will follow.

Think about the financial implications. A word to the men. Do you know what this divorce is going to cost you? Do you think your bravado and bluster is going to impress the courts? The financial costs can be crippling. Not only will there always be maintenance responsibilities if children are involved, but there is the emotional stress of having your financial commitment challenged and changed from time to time. This stress is aggravated if you remarry and have an additional family to care for.

How unnecessary if it can all be avoided. And it can be! With the right help and patience on your part, God can do wonderful things. He has done it for others, why not for you? Ask yourself whether you really have a biblical warrant for a divorce. Do you really and truly have a good reason to go through with it – or are you just angry and proud?

Think about marriage. It is not simply a voluntary agreement the two of you entered into and which you can abandon whenever you please. Go back to chapter 7. Marriage is not merely sentiment. On the contrary, the Bible's view of marriage is far higher than that. It is seen as a covenant. In biblical days covenants were very serious matters. God Himself enters into a covenant with us when we become Christians. It is a serious and a binding agreement.

Marriage is a covenant of companionship (Mal. 2:13-14). Marriage is not primarily about the privileges of sex or the begetting and rearing of children. It is about companionship. The wife described as a 'helper suitable for him' (Gen. 2:18). A helper! Not only that, but a helper suitable for him. What a gift from a gracious God! Don't throw it away.

Have you understood your roles?

Many a family squabble could have been avoided if the members of the family knew where they fitted in. In no area can life be lived happily without rules and roles. We are designed that way. We work and live in community with others. We all need to know what our role is and the family is no different.

The family has come under severe attack in recent years. Vociferous lobby groups have scornfully derided the traditional family of husband, wife and children. In frenzied attempts to prove that alternative lifestyles are acceptable and normal, we have seen the promotion of homosexual relationships, one-parent families, women deliberately conceiving children out of wedlock so that the joy of having a child may be experienced even though the child's joy of having a live-in traditional father is ignored. What is the end result of all of this? Take a look around you.

Homeless children, rude and arrogant behaviour, irresponsible men, struggling mothers, materialistic teenagers, test-tube babies with all the ethical problems now surfacing, the blurring of the lines between right and wrong, and hundreds of other sociological problems that cause stress, not happiness.

Do you think the alternatives to the traditional family are working? Is it not possible that at least part of the problem in your own home is because the two of you got married without the foggiest idea of how it is all supposed to work? God has given us His rules for the happy functioning of a family. When they are observed, they really do work.

The Bible makes the man the head of the family. This is not superiority but rather a function. As we know, we cannot all be chiefs. There can be only one chief in the family. God has placed the responsibility for this upon the man. The Israelite family was patriarchal. Genealogical lines of families were always traced according to the father's line, never the mother's line – not because the mothers were unimportant, but simply because God places the responsibility for the family first and foremost upon the father.

The man's first responsibility is the *tender care of his wife*. In Ephesians 5:28 husbands are told to love their wives as they love their own bodies. As they would act instinctively to protect themselves from danger, injury, hurt or discomfort, so they should act instinctively to protect their wives. In 1 Peter 3:7 the same point is made when Peter, writing under the inspiration of the Holy Spirit, says:

> Husbands, in the same way be considerate as you live with your wives, and treat them with respect ... so that nothing will hinder your prayers.

Husbands, your relationship with God could well depend on how you are treating your wife.

The second function God has placed upon the man as head of the home is to *provide for his family*. In 1 Timothy 5:8 we have a very interesting reference. The apostle Paul, writing to Timothy, says that a man must provide for his family and if he doesn't do this, 'he has denied the faith'. Paul says that a man who refuses to provide for his family has denied the faith. This is not a reference to a man who is unable to do so through circumstances or has failed even though he has honestly tried. In other words a man who will not provide for this family in a consistent and responsible manner cannot be regarded as a Christian.

Thirdly, the main responsibility for *instructing children in the ways of God*, the pathways of righteousness and the truths of salvation lies with the father – not with the mother. It is not that the mother does not have any responsibility in this regard. On the contrary, the father cannot do it alone, but *accountability* lies with the father.

This is illustrated in the Bible by placing the role of family priest upon the man. Examples of this may be found in Genesis 8:20, 12:7-8, 22:2-9, and in Exodus 12. Every now and then, the head of the home had to set up an altar and represent his family before God. Men have to act as pastors and priests to their own families. The spiritual care of the children cannot entirely be left to the church or even to the wife.

I realise that there are a thousand other things that could be said and taken into account. I am aware that there are sincere men who try very hard to bring godliness into their families but have wives who just will not co-operate or submit to the commandments of God and the role they ought to play in their homes. The commandment puts fathers first, underscoring the truth that headship rests with the father.

There must be order in the home, and my concern is that often a marriage may be in difficulty simply because the people concerned have not been helped in putting it all together. Could this possibly be true of you?

It does not need to be this way. Is it too late for your marriage? Is there still room for help? If you are struggling with the decision whether to pursue a divorce, may I ask if you have taken into account the problems caused by a blurring of roles in the family? If this is a factor, I urge you to reconsider. These things can be remedied by God's grace. Don't allow your family to disintegrate because of things that can be changed.

Have you understood the dynamics of a marriage relationship?

There are certain things which are absolutely necessary for a relationship to grow. The obvious things include the need to communicate and share with each other – the need to verbalise and engage in conversation. There is the need for tenderness, touching, the demonstration of love and affection, little ways of showing appreciation to each other. There is the need for patience, for listening, for budgeting time with each other. There is the need to understand how important friendships are to women, the need for them to talk and share their feelings with their own sex.

All these needs and many more go into that mysterious thing we call 'a marriage relationship'. But there is something more that we should note – the need to accept each other as we are. We need to understand the pressures and difficulties the other faces, and to make allowance for the different thresholds we all have for coping with the stresses and strains of living. We are not all the same and the stress fractures in each of us are often hidden deep from the prying eyes of others. Yet we all have a threshold that, when crossed, makes life unbearable.

Stephen Langley was a good hard-working man who lived a comfortable middle-class lifestyle. He had been married to the same person for twenty-three years. One day he made a loan from the bank of £1,200. In spite of financial difficulties, he paid back most of it. He was, however, £72 in the red. He received two letters from the bank.

What do you think he did? How important is £72? Did he stalk into the bank and blow his top? No. Did he go home and have an argument with his wife? No. Did he simply get angry and sulk? No. A line in Stephen's mind had been crossed. The stress was too great. He gassed himself in his car. He left a note that said: 'I just can't go on handling the pressure of simply living' (*The Weekly Telegraph*, Issue no. 137, p. 204).

A paltry £72! But the pressure was too great. And so it is with us in our relationships as well. Pressures may build up and finally a seemingly petty thing causes a massive reaction. A hidden threshold has been crossed. Let's be aware of the pressures on our partners.

Dr James Dobson has a timely word in his book *Straight Talk* for both husbands and wives.

Let me say it more directly. For the man who appreciates the willingness of his wife to stand against the tide of public opinion – staying at home in her empty neighbourhood in the exclusive company of jelly-faced toddlers and strong-willed adolescents – it is about time you gave her some help. I'm not merely suggesting that you wash the dishes or sweep the floor. I'm referring to the provision of emotional support ... of conversation ... of making her feel like a lady ... of building her ego ... of giving her one day of recreation each week ... of taking her out to dinner ... of telling her that you love her. Without these armaments, she is left defenceless against the foes of the family – the foes of *your* family!

But to be honest, many of you husbands and fathers have been thinking about something else. Your wives have been busy attending seminars and reading family literature and studying the Bible, but they can't even get you to enter a discussion about what they've learned. You've been intoxicated with your work and the ego support it provides.

So much for the men! But wives too need to accept their husbands as they are. Dr Dobson's advice to women is:

My strongest words are addressed to the wife of a good man, whom we will call Fred. He loves Barbara and the kids. Honest! He would literally lay down his life for them if required. He doesn't drink. He has never smoked. He has no compulsion to gamble. He wouldn't touch another woman under any imaginable circumstances. He gets up every morning and plods off to work, perhaps holding down a boring, menial job for forty-five years. He brings his salary home and does his best to stretch it through the month. He lives by a moral code that is remarkable for this dishonest era. His income tax return is scrupulously accurate, and he's never stolen so much as a paper clip from his boss. He doesn't beat the kids or kick the dog or flirt with the widow next door. He is as predictable as the sunrise, and I'm sure that God has a special place for him on the other side.

But Steady Freddie has a serious flaw. He was raised in a day when little boys were taught to withhold their thoughts and feelings. 'Children are to be seen and not heard,' said his parents. He can't remember being hugged or praised, and everybody knows that boys don't cry. So Fred learned his lessons well. He became as tough as nails and as silent as the night, but in so doing, he lost touch with his emotions. Now, he *cannot* be spontaneous and affectionate, no matter how hard he tries. It just isn't within him. And most of his thoughts remain unspoken and private.

One would hope that Barbara would accept Fred as he is, since she knew his nature before they were married. In fact it was his quiet reserve that made Fred attractive to her when they were courting. He always seemed so strong, so in control, compared to her impulsive flightiness. But now Barbara is fed up with her unromantic husband. She is deeply angry because he won't communicate with her, and she nags him incessantly about his alleged 'failures' as a husband. He can do *nothing* right and she makes them both miserable year after year.

The point is that divorce is not always necessary. Get your family into perspective. Don't give up hope too quickly. Make sure every avenue has been explored before you turn to the very last resort.

Have you exercised forgiveness?
Let us assume that your problems are really big. You have

been badly hurt by your partner's actions. No one denies the pain and anger, especially if your partner has been unfaithful. But assuming the unfaithfulness or whatever it was that caused you think about divorce – assuming that there has been true repentance, have you tried forgiveness?

Forgiveness is ultimately the only way we can handle broken relationships. It is the only way we can lay past problems to rest. Forgiveness is not a surge of emotion. It is a deliberate act of the will. For the Christian, the forgiveness we exercise is based on the fact that we ourselves have been forgiven by God.

I know that many hurting partners will say, 'I have forgiven again and again.' If that is so and your forgiveness has been abused and trampled on, it may well be time for other action. But before you take that final step, put all your problems into perspective. Is it worth throwing away the past years if it is possible to salvage the relationship with an act of Christian forgiveness?

I am not suggesting it is easy. Nor am I suggesting that the pain will mysteriously go away or that all the problems will be sorted out overnight. There may be a great deal of work that needs to be done.

In his best-selling book *The Freedom of Forgiveness* David Augsberger writes:

> Bitterness is a cyclical, repetitive, tightly closed circle of self-centred pain. It carries us around and around the same senseless arc, around and around ourselves. Like a child learning to ride a bicycle, knowing how to ride but not how to stop, we pedal on and on, afraid to quit, yet wishing desperately for someone to come and take the bars, break our circling, and let us off. Bitterness is

useless. Repayment is impossible. Revenge is impotent. Resentment is impractical.

Only forgiveness can reconcile the differences and restore healing to a relationship. Rejecting all relationships that have failed us is the most common 'solution' in our contemporary Western culture, among Christians and non-Christians alike. Cut off the old connections, withdraw from all interactions, live at a distance, avoid intimacy or involvement. Above all, do not risk working at forgiveness.

Common as this option is, it is destructive of human relationships, it fragments personality, it is inconsistent with the basic values of any faith commitment.

Only if you have no need for forgiveness yourself do you dare consider hesitating to forgive another. The two go hand in hand.

'If you forgive other people their failures, your Heavenly Father will also forgive you. But if you will not forgive ... neither will your Heavenly Father forgive you your failures' (Matt. 6:14-15).

'I'll never forgive,' General James Oglethorpe said to John Wesley.

'Then I hope, sir,' replied Wesley, 'you never sin!' (pp.17-18).

No, it's not easy to forgive and it is impossible to forget. But it is nevertheless possible to forgive because we as believers have the power of the Holy Spirit within. All I ask now as you try to get things into perspective is this: have you done it? Have you considered forgiveness?

Have you faced up to your need of Christ?
Knowing Christ personally is the dynamic all of us need

in our lives. We may say we are Christians when in fact it is not true. We may think we are Christians but be mistaken. We may genuinely believe in Christ but somehow, in the hurt and trauma of marriage breakdown, we lose contact with Him. Speaking about forgiveness inevitably brings us back to our need for God in our lives.

Does your marriage have any spiritual foundations at all? Has He who ordained marriage been left out? Has the thought that your home needs God ever entered your mind? Perhaps this is the time for you to meet the only One who is able to save your marriage and heal the hurts and the pain in your life.

Let me introduce you, then, to the ultimate hope for those who are hurting.

CHAPTER 16

The ultimate hope for the hurting

Why are we as we are? What dark and secret power is at work within us that makes it impossible to get on with each other? Are we doomed by forces outside our control never to know the certainty, happiness and security of a stable marriage?

If we are to believe a bizarre article in *Time* magazine (August 1994), we are indeed caught in the grip of an unseen force – our own genes. According to this report with the tantalizing title 'Our Cheating Hearts', certain researchers have concluded that the reason we are unfaithful to each other is not moral but rather biological:

> Of course you don't need a Ph.D. to see that till-death-do-us-part fidelity doesn't come as naturally to people as say, eating. But an emerging field known as evolutionary psychology can now put a finer point on the matter. By studying how the process of natural selection shaped the mind, evolutionary psychologists are painting a new portrait of human nature with fresh detail about the feelings and thoughts that draw us into marriage – and push us out (p. 43).

The problem really lies in our genes, the article argues, and lifelong monogamous devotion just isn't natural. Is all this true? Fortunately it is not. There really is hope for the hurting. That hope lies in God and the magnificent life-transforming grace which is ours because Christ died on the cross and rose again on the third day.

'But how does this help me?' you may ask. 'What has this got to do with what is happening in my home right now?' Let us answer these questions.

Defining the real problem

Behind all marital discord lies a profound problem that needs to be faced. The problem is not merely rooted in a few misconceptions but is deeply embedded in human nature itself. It is the problem of sin. Not sins (plural) but sin (singular).

The Bible teaches that there is a dark principle at work within us. There is something drastically wrong with us on the inside. We are sinners. This is the cause of all the hurtful things we do to each other. The fruits of our human nature are bitter and destructive. These are sins (plural), that we struggle with day by day.

To illustrate this, let us look at a portion of Scripture which describes human nature. The apostle Paul writes in Romans 3:10-18:

> As it is written:
> 'There is no one righteous, not even one;
>> there is no one who understands,
>> no one who seeks God.
> All have turned away,
>> they have together become worthless;
> there is no one who does good,
>> not even one.'

'Their throats are open graves;
  their tongues practise deceit.'
'The poison of vipers is on their lips.'
  'Their mouths are full of cursing and bitterness.'
'Their feet are swift to shed blood;
  ruin and misery mark their ways,
and the way of peace they do not know.'
  'There is no fear of God before their eyes.'

In these verses Paul collates a number of Old Testament references to describe human nature as it really is. He does this to show us that we are unable to do anything to redeem ourselves and that we need a Saviour. But in the process he shows us what the human heart is really like and why we treat each other as we do. Notice the list:

- No one is righteous – not one (v. 10).
- No one understands the human plight or bothers to seek God (v. 11).
- All have turned away from God and thus all human endeavours at earning God's approval are worthless (v. 12).
- A repetition, that not one of us is good by nature (v. 12).
- Our throats, tongues and lips, i.e. the organs we use to communicate, are filled with death (graves), deceit and poison (v. 13).
- Our mouths are full of malice (v. 14).
- Violence is part of our lifestyle (v. 15).
- As a result of their pointless, futile and directionless living, most people's lives are full of misery and personal ruin (v. 16).

- They have no peace, harmony or inner prosperity (v. 17).
- They have no fear, awe or respect for God (v. 18).

This is the cause of all their problems.

Is this not a picture of many people today? Is it not at least partly true of what you have experienced in your own home? Those awful human traits are only too familiar to us – instead of innate human goodness, we are filled with lies, deceit, malice, anger and bitterness. This all too often leads to verbal or physical abuse. The end result is a constant source of misery and discontent.

Where does all this come from? Let us turn to the wisest man who ever lived for the answer – our Lord Jesus Christ Himself:

> For from within, out of men's hearts, come evil thoughts, sexual immorality, theft, murder, adultery, greed, malice, deceit, lewdness, envy, slander, arrogance and folly. All these evils come from inside and make a man unclean (Mark 7:21-23).

The problem of unfaithfulness lies in the heart. The ability we have to hurt and deceive each other is rooted in human nature itself. This does not mean that everyone is as evil as it is possible to be. Nor does it mean that marriage and human relationships are doomed from the start. We all know of people who are happily married, many who may have no Christian connection at all.

A great many controlling factors operate in our lives. For example, we all have different temperaments, family backgrounds, values that we have grown up with that influence our actions and reactions. However the potential for great evil lies within all our hearts and, as the Bible consistently testifies, we are all sinners. There is no one who by nature, left to himself, would automatically seek God.

Thus when family conflict breaks out and great harm is caused and a potential divorce is threatening, we need to remember where it is all coming from – our evil hearts. This does not mean that the innocent party in the divorce action is guilty of the sinful actions of his or her partner. But it helps the hurting victim to know that the reason for the lies, deceit and betrayal is not because he or she has done something wrong, but simply because their spouse wanted to do it.

This is something that needs to be borne in mind because often the hurting partner wants to know what they have done wrong. Without suggesting that they are perfect, I often have to remind such people that they in fact may have done nothing wrong whatever. Their partner has simply given in to the passions and dictates of a sinful nature.

How does this affect our homes?

How does the fact that we have sinful natures work out in our domestic lives? How does it contribute to the break-up of the home? The answer is that sin makes us all *self-centred*. Our own interests and comfort become the controlling factors in our lives.

This is illustrated in many ways in the Bible. Take for instance the story of Cain and Abel. Cain killed Abel because he was jealous and angry. The Scripture describes him like this: 'his face was downcast' (Gen. 4:5). He was depressed because his brother succeeded where he failed. John tells us that Cain 'belonged to the evil one.' He murdered his brother simply because his brother's deeds were righteous (1 John 3:12).

Satan used this dynamic of self-centredness as an allegation against Job when God confronted him. In Job 1:9-11 we read:

> 'Does Job fear God for nothing?' Satan replied. 'Have you not put a hedge around him and his household and everything he has? You have blessed the work of his hands, so that his flocks and herds are spread throughout the land. But stretch out your hand and strike everything he has, and he will surely curse you to your face.'

Selfishness is a very powerful force. Hence Paul's exhortation to us in various New Testament passages. Take for example his words in Ephesians 4:31-32:

> Get rid of all bitterness, rage and anger, brawling and slander, along with every form of malice. Be kind and compassionate to one another, forgiving each other, just as in Christ God forgave you.

Or his words in Philippians 2:3-7:

> Do nothing out of selfish ambition or vain conceit, but in humility consider others better than yourselves. Each of you should look not only to your own interests, but also to the interests of others.
>
> Your attitude should be the same as that of Christ Jesus:
>
> Who, being in very nature God,
> did not consider equality with God
> something to be grasped,
> but made himself nothing,
> taking the very nature of a servant,
> being made in human likeness.

We could also refer to Paul's great definitions of love in 1 Corinthians 13 and the fruit of the Spirit in Galatians 5:22-23. One of the fruits of the Spirit of God indwelling us is 'self-control'. Why self-control? Exactly because our natures are given to self-expression, self-aggrandisement and self-satisfaction. All too often we let our self-interest rule us and dominate our actions.

This is what happens in a marriage that is distintegrating. One partner, if not both, has opted for self-centredness and is determined to have his or her way. Think about it for a moment. All those arguments, tiffs, disagreements, sulks, periods of silence and aloofness – what are they really? They are ways in which we try to get our own way.

When your partner says, 'I don't love you any more,' he or she is really saying, 'I love me most of all. I want my needs met.' When they say, 'You don't understand me. We got married too young,' they are really saying, 'The most important person in the world is me, my happiness and wellbeing. You've become a hindrance and a nuisance.'

All the arguments and disagreements that result in broken relationships and disharmony are the result of self-centredness, which is the consequence of sin.

Marriage problems are often attributed to past circumstances, such as domineering parents who may have unduly influenced the decision to marry. Whatever the truth of such allegations, blame-shifting is the mark of a self-centred person. It's always some else's fault. Sin makes us selfish.

Every expression of anger in your home; every event that has caused heartache and disappointment; every lie and deception; every expression of abuse; every act of recklessness; gambling, violence; every tear that has been shed; every depression that has been caused, is someone saying *I am more important than anyone else*. Never forget that all marriage problems are caused by selfishness – and selfishness is caused by sin.

What is the answer?

The answer lies in the Christian gospel. God sent His Son into the world to die for us on the cross. He paid for our sins. And He rose again from the grave to announce His victory over death for all time. He is the only Person in the universe who can help us because He is divine and has divine power. More than that, He can help us because He was also human and understands us:

> For we do not have a high priest who is unable to sympathise with our weaknesses, but we have one who has been tempted in every way, just as we are – yet was without sin. Let us then approach the throne of grace with confidence, so that we may receive mercy and find grace to help us in our time of need (Heb. 4:15-16).

But how can He help me? The first thing is to make sure you know Him. That's the secret. Many people pray, but they are praying to a God they do not know. Jesus can help us to know God. In fact the Bible teaches us that He actually imparts the authority to us to become children of God (John 1:11-13).

We do not become children of God in the sense that all people everywhere are sometimes thought to be God's children universally. Rather, we become His children in a personal, intimate way. We are adopted into His family. Our sins are all forgiven and we receive a new nature.

Let us pause for a moment to discuss this new nature. Herein lies the answer we so desperately need for our ailing marriages, relationships and hearts. What does it mean when we talk about a 'new creation' (2 Cor. 5:17)? It means simply that the tendency to self-centredness has been tackled at its root. Instead we now have the potential to respond to others as our Lord Jesus himself did.

He was not *self-centred* but *other person centred*. Everything He did, He did for others. He illustrated this for us the evening before He was crucified. In John's Gospel chapter 13 we have the amazing account of Jesus washing His disciples' feet. He explains His action to His disciples in verses 13-17:

> You call me 'Teacher' and 'Lord', and rightly so, for that is what I am. Now that I, your Lord and Teacher, have washed your feet, you also should wash one another's feet. I have set you an example that you should do as I have done for you. I tell you the truth, no servant is greater than his master, nor is a messenger greater than the one who sent him. Now that you know these things, you will be blessed if you do them.

Can you see how this affects your relationships? If you were concerned about your partner instead of yourself, and your partner was equally concerned about you, what harmony, love, security and warmth there would be. Many people enter marriage with the idea that it is a fifty-fifty deal. If you produce your fifty, I will produce mine and all will work out. But this is wrong because it implies that if you do not produce your fifty, my commitment to you goes out of the window.

This unrealistic view explains why marriage so often

fails today. Our attitude should be: 'I commit myself 100% to you, without reservation, to serve your best interests for the rest of my life. If you do the same for me, we have the ingredients for harmony, love, and a future together.' But this kind of philosophy, this kind of selflessness, can only be imparted by Christ. He and He alone can change the human heart. He can give us a second chance.

If you are not yet divorced

How does all this help you if your marriage is pretty far gone but the divorce has not yet been finalised? I know that each situation is different and it may well be that the situation has gone too far to be reversed. You and your spouse may have seen marriage counsellors with no positive result. But there is always hope when we come to Christ. Have you turned to Jesus Christ?

If only one of you turns to Christ while the other persists in going his or her own way, there is not much anyone can do except to pray for the erring partner. But often there is a secret longing to reverse the process of divorce. Secret regrets eat away at our hearts, and we long to retrace our steps, to relive our lives and avoid the mistakes.

If that is how you both feel, there is hope. You must come before Jesus Christ and receive Him. When He comes into your life, He brings with Him His power to change. Behaviour *can* change; selfishness *can* be banished; a new other-person-oriented nature *is* possible.

Christian pastors and counsellors around the world could tell of the changes wrought in marriages when Christ becomes Lord. Your divorce is not necessary – unless there are extreme circumstances referred to elsewhere in this book. It is possible to change. Christ can bring hope – even to those who are hurting and in pain because of huge disappointments in their marriage.

What if it is too late for my marriage?

Sometimes the trauma of the marriage breakdown and the subsequent divorce opens people up to Jesus Christ for the first time. It is not always possible to stop the divorce from happening. It is true that sometimes the lonely road of hurt and pain has to be endured. But can Christ do anything for you?

You must realise that a divorce with its accompanying hurt can obscure a greater need in your life – your need of a Saviour. Even if your marriage worked out and was extremely happy, you would still need a Saviour. The divorce sometimes simply lays bare the fact that our lives have no foundation – we have no real inner resources.

The first thing you need to be aware of is that, through your tears and pain, you have a need of God. You do not need Him merely to ease the hurt, to take away the fear or to reverse the situation. You need Him because, like all of us, you are a sinner who needs a Saviour.

Often the person who is hurting finds it hard to come to terms with this because they have been so sinned against. It may take time for their great spiritual need to become clear. But it is a real need. You do need a Saviour and the only Saviour is Christ (Acts 4:12). You must make sure of your relationship to Him. Do you know Him? Have you ever really come to Him? If not, why not take a few minutes of quiet reflection to do so now.

You may wonder how to do this. How does someone 'come' to Christ? What do you have to do or say?

Prayer of faith

There is only one way in which we can come to Christ, and that is by faith. There is only one way in which we can bring our hearts to Him, and that is through prayer. Coming to Christ entails more than a simple prayer of repentance. We need to surrender our whole being in glad and willing allegiance to Him. It is, quite literally, a case of a life for a life – Christ's abundant life for the surrender of our impoverished, sinful lives.

Take your Bible and find a quiet place where you can be undisturbed for a few minutes.

- Using your own words, tell God how you truly feel about yourself. Tell Him that He is right and that you are wrong; that you are a sinner worthy only of judgement. Admit the sins and failures in your life one by one. Do not excuse yourself. Verbalise your confession to God, starting with the words, 'Oh God, I come before You now ...'

- Tell God that you believe that Jesus died for you on the cross. Admit that, although you do not understand it all, you know that His death paid the price for your sins. Acknowledge that you are unworthy of this, but that you are glad Jesus died for you.

- Now tell God that you wish to turn from all unbelief and sin and that you long to trust in Christ to receive eternal life. Admit that you cannot have forgiveness or eternal life apart from His grace and mercy. Starting with the words, 'O God, have mercy on me ...' ask God for forgiveness.

- Offer your life to God. Tell Him that you no longer

want to be ruled by pride, but that you wish to surrender to Him, your Lord and King. Ask Him to receive you as a member of His family. Promise that, as long as He gives you the strength, you will live for Him and trust Him.

- Now turn to John 6:37 and read Jesus' promise. He will not turn away anyone who comes to Him. Tell God that you are coming to Him on the basis of what Jesus did for you on the cross. Remind Him that He has promised not to turn you away and that you trust His Word. Put your finger on the verse and say: 'O God, I trust Your promise, given by Your Son, that none will be turned away.' Believe what Jesus says. Put your faith in Him and decide consciously to trust Him with your eternal destiny.

- Thank Him for providing such a great salvation for you and for this opportunity to turn to Him. Express your gratitude that He has heard your prayer.[1]

You may want to make a list of the things that are bothering you most, for discussion with a trusted minister or Christian friend. Certain things may need to change in your life. Think about them and write them down too for discussion with a counsellor or minister.

Your surrender to Christ is this way is the most important thing that you will ever do. Even if your marriage difficulties with the emotional aftermath seem to overshadow everything else, nothing can compare in importance with coming to Christ.

---

1.   *Finding God*, pp. 70-2

Can Christ heal my hurts?

The answer to that is 'yes'. I do not mean to suggest that He will miraculously take all the hurts away. The ache may be with you for some time, as will some of the practical problems you face. But let me list some of the ways you can expect Christ's help in your hurt.

Firstly, as you grow spiritually, you will increasingly *understand* what went wrong in your marriage. You will understand more about human nature and its bent towards self-centredness and evil. You will slowly get things into perspective and be able to cope with your feelings.

Secondly, Christ has promised *His special presence* to all His children when they go through trials and difficulties. Turn again to Isaiah 43:1-2:

> But now, this is what the LORD says –
>> he who created you, O Jacob,
>> he who formed you, O Israel:
> 'Fear not, for I have redeemed you;
>> I have summoned you by name, you are mine.
> When you pass through the waters,
>> I will be with you;
> and when you pass through the rivers,
>> they will not sweep over you.
> When you walk through the fire,
>> you will not be burned;
>> the flames will not set you ablaze.'

When you pass through the waters! That is what is happening to you now. It may continue to be a tough battle for some time. But God promises His people: 'I will be with you.' The problem is that we want to feel His presence. We want tangible evidence, both emotionally and circumstantially, that He is there. While this is sometimes the case, it is not always so. As we *trust Him*, we discover that, miraculously, we are making it through!

Thirdly, Christ promises us *His protection* and provision. Think of the Shepherd God of Psalm 23 or the great Protector in Psalm 91. Turn to the Good Shepherd of John 10:1-18. Read these passages and see what they say. Then turn to our wonderful Lord's promises of provision in Matthew 6:25-34.

While it is true there may be some struggle in store; that we must work to earn a living; that it is hard to make ends meet, especially if you have children to support; that the evenings can be very lonely – He is there. We do not need to panic the way unbelievers do (v. 32). We have a Father in Heaven, we have a Saviour on the throne, who is a Friend and a Brother to us.

Fourthly, once you become a Christian and become part of a Christian fellowship, it is not long before you develop a *new circle of friends*. Support groups are necessary. They can be dangerous if their values are wrong and you could be pressurised into doing things that will further complicate your life. But to have a group of people around you who believe what you do, who love the same Saviour and are committed to the same values, is a source of great strength and security. This kind of friendship is found within the fellowship of a church. Here you will be loved, prayed for and supported.

Finally, as you follow Christ, you will find yourself undergoing all kinds of wonderful and positive *changes*. You will settle down after a while. Most people who go through a divorce do in fact survive.

I am not pretending that it is easy. Divorce is not

a trivial thing. The effects of the divorce may linger for years. Some people never quite overcome the hurt and trauma. Their loss of self-confidence may haunt them for years. But it is equally true that most people eventually succeed in picking up the pieces and begin a new life. That will in all likelihood happen to you.

As a Christian, you will find additional changes taking place. You will find your faith in Christ growing and a sense of confidence and self-worth returning. You will find a new significance for yourself because of your relationship with Him. Your values and perspectives will change. A new sense of purpose will quietly settle on you. Your life will take a new direction with spiritual objectives as your goals.

If and when a new relationship develops, you will be better able to assess things. You will have new foundations on which to build because the great doctrines and principles of God's Word will take root in your life. They will give you insight and understanding you did not have before. You will find Psalm 119:130 absolutely true: 'The unfolding of your words gives light.' You will discover that God's Word truly becomes 'a lamp to my feet and a light for my path' (v. 105).

Yes, once you become a Christian you do change. And best of all, God is with you in all the years that lie ahead. He promised:

'Never will I leave you;
never will I forsake you.'
(Heb. 13:5)

He is indeed the only ultimate hope for all those who are hurting.

Bibliography

Adams, Jay E. *Christian Living in the Home*, Grand Rapids, Baker Book House, 1972

    The Christian Counsellor's Manual, Grand Rapids, Baker Book House, 1973

    Competent to Counsel, Phillipsburg, Presbyterian and Reformed, 1975

    Marriage, Divorce and Remarriage, Phillipsburg, Presbyterian and Reformed, 1980

Augsberger, David. *The Freedom of Forgiveness*, Chicago, Moody Press, 1988

Berry, Jo. *Beloved Unbeliever*, Grand Rapids, Zondervan Publishing House, 1981

Charnock, Stephen. *Existence and Attributes of God*, Grand Rapids, Baker Book House, 1986

Christenson, Larry. *The Christian Family*, Minneapolis, Bethany Fellowship, 1970

Collins, Gary. *Christian Counselling*, Milton Keynes, Word UK, 1980

Crabbe, Lawrence J., Jr. *The Marriage Builder*, Grand Rapids, Zondervan Publishing House, 1982

Danby, Herbert. *Mishnah: Translated from Hebrew*, London, Oxford University Press, 1933

Dobash, R. Emerson and Russell Dobash. *Violence Against Wives*, London, Open Books, 1980

Dobson, James C. *What Wives Wish Their Husbands Knew About Women*, Wheaton, Tyndale House, 1981

Love Must Be Tough, Eastbourne, Kingsway Publications, 1983

Straight Talk, Cape Town, Struik Christian Books, 1991

Hart, Nicky. *When Marriage Ends*, Cambridge, Tavistock Publications, 1976

Knox, D. Broughton. *The Everlasting God*, Homebush West, Lancer Books, 1988

Lloyd-Jones, D. Martyn. *Studies in the Sermon on the Mount*, London, Inter-Varsity Fellowship, 1959, volume 1

Mace, David R. *Hebrew Marriage*, London, Epworth Press, 1953

Minirth, Frank B. and Paul D. Meier. *Happiness is a Choice*, Grand Rapids, Baker Book House, 1978

Moore, Donna M. *Battered Women*, California, Sage Publishers, 1979

Murray, John. *Principles of Conduct*, London, Tyndale Press, 1957

Divorce, Phillipsburg, Presbyterian and Reformed, 1961

Powers, B. Ward. *Marriage and Divorce: The New Testament Teaching*, Concorde: Family Life Movement of Australia, 1987

Retief, Frank. *Finding God*, Cape Town, Struik Christian Books/ Milton Keynes, Nelson Word, 1994

Tragedy to Triumph, Cape Town, Struik Christian Books/ Milton Keynes, Nelson Word, 1994

Richmond, Gary. *The Divorce Decision*, Dallas, Word Publishing, 1988

Rushdoony, Rousas John. *The Institutes of Biblical Law*, Phillipsburg, P & R Publishing, 1973

'Law and Society', in *The Institutes of Biblical Law*, Volume II, Vallecito, Ross House Books, 1986

Sutton, Ray R. *Second Chance, Biblical Hope for the Divorced*, Fort Worth, Dominion Press, 1988

Vincent, M.O. *God, Sex and You*, London, Scripture Union, 1971

Vincent, Marvin R. *Word Studies in the New Testament*, Grand Rapids, Eerdmans, 1957

Vine, W.E. *An Expository Dictionary of New Testament Words*, London, Oliphants, 1963

Christian Focus Publications
publishes books for all ages

Our mission statement –

STAYING FAITHFUL
In dependence upon God we seek to impact the world through literature faithful to His infallible Word, the Bible. Our aim is to ensure that the LORD Jesus Christ is presented as the only hope to obtain forgiveness of sin, live a useful life and look forward to heaven with Him.

REACHING OUT
Christ's last command requires us to reach out to our world with His gospel. We seek to help fulfil that by publishing books that point people towards Jesus and help them develop a Christ-like maturity. We aim to equip all levels of readers for life, work, ministry and mission.

Books in our adult range are published in three imprints.

Christian Focus contains popular works including biographies, commentaries, basic doctrine and Christian living. Our children's books are also published in this imprint.

Mentor focuses on books written at a level suitable for Bible College and seminary students, pastors, and other serious readers. The imprint includes commentaries, doctrinal studies, examination of current issues and church history.

Christian Heritage contains classic writings from the past.

Christian Focus Publications Ltd,
Geanies House, Fearn, Ross-shire,
IV20 1TW, Scotland, United Kingdom
info@christianfocus.com
www.christianfocus.com